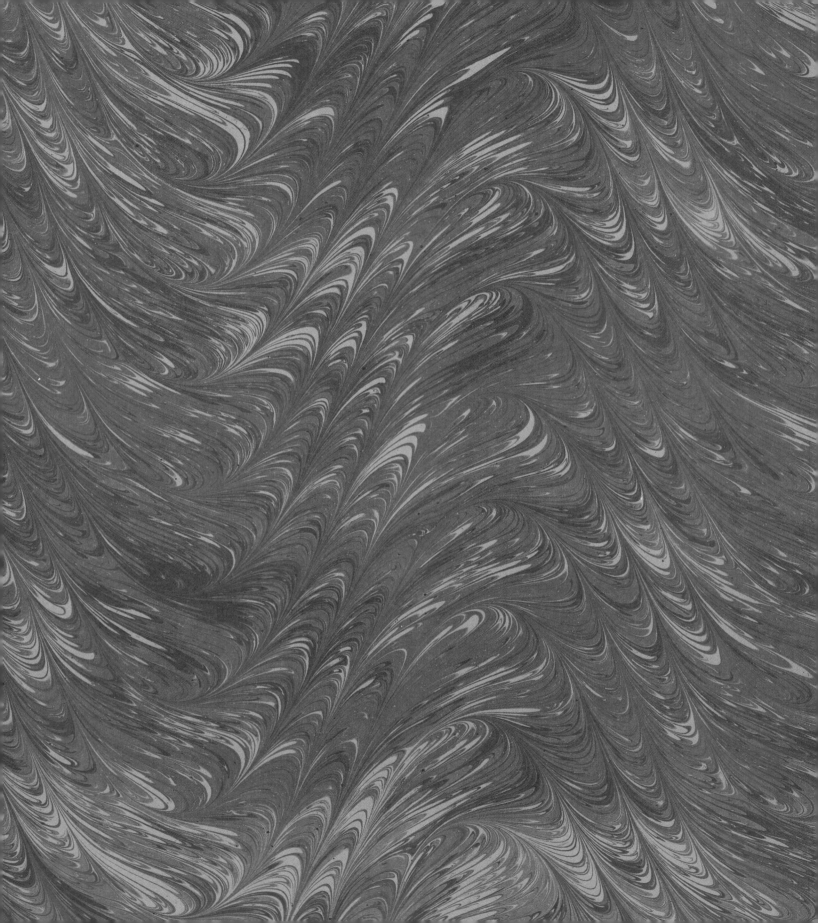

HARCOURT

TROPHIES

A HARCOURT READING/LANGUAGE ARTS PROGRAM

GATHER AROUND

SENIOR AUTHORS
Isabel L. Beck ◆ Roger C. Farr ◆ Dorothy S. Strickland

AUTHORS
Alma Flor Ada ◆ Marcia Brechtel ◆ Margaret McKeown
Nancy Roser ◆ Hallie Kay Yopp

SENIOR CONSULTANT
Asa G. Hilliard III

CONSULTANTS
F. Isabel Campoy ◆ David A. Monti

Harcourt

Orlando Boston Dallas Chicago San Diego

Visit *The Learning Site!*

www.harcourtschool.com

Acknowledgments appear in the back of this book.

Printed in the United States of America

ISBN 0-15-335588-3

2 3 4 5 6 7 8 9 10 048 10 09 08 07 06 05 04 03

HARCOURT

TROPHIES

A HARCOURT READING/LANGUAGE ARTS PROGRAM

GATHER AROUND

Dear Reader,

Gather Around for some terrific stories! In this book, you will learn to be a detective. You will also meet a brave little bird, a baby baboon, and a very silly pig. Like some of the characters in these stories, you may be surprised by what you find. So, turn the page and let the adventure begin!

Sincerely,

The Authors

The Authors

THEME 6

Going Places

CONTENTS

Theme Big Books

Decodable Books 27-34

THEME 6

Going Places

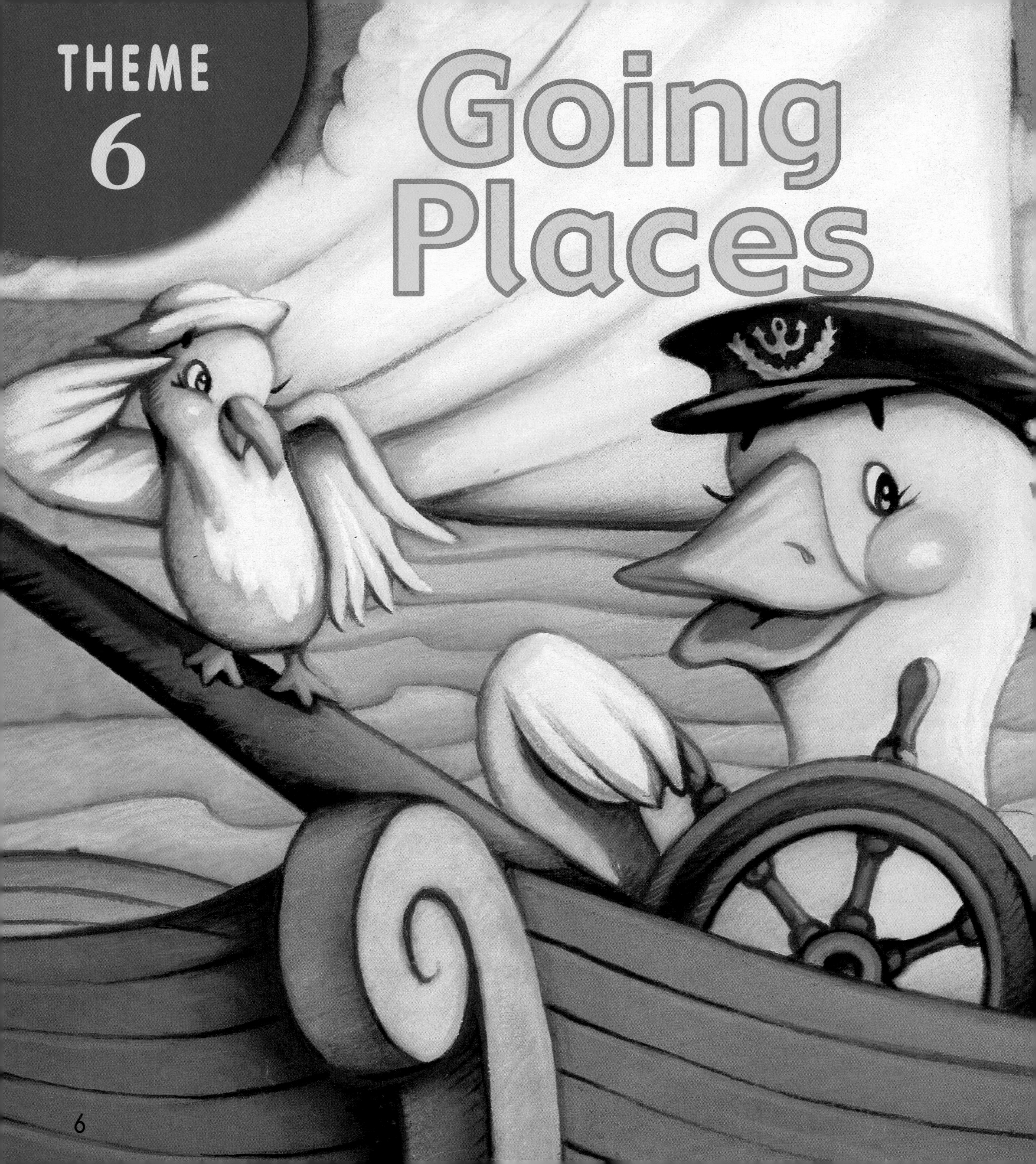

▲ The Story of a Blue Bird

Word Power

Words to Remember

afraid

flew

join

learn

nothing

thought

wonder

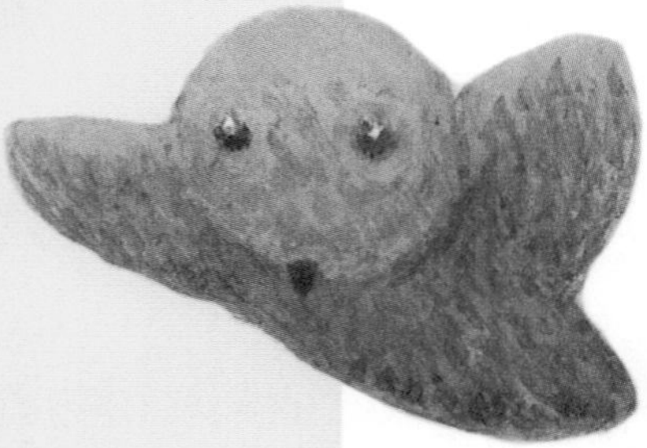

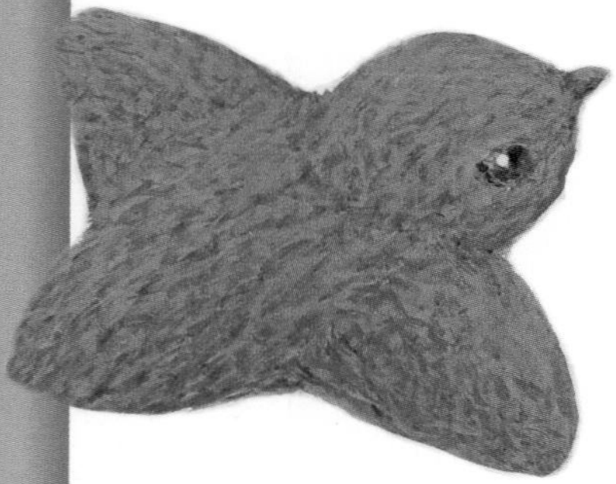

"I **wonder** what flying is like," **thought** the little blue bird. His mother **flew** down to the nest. She said, "It's time for you to **learn** to fly. Go and **join** the other birds. There's **nothing** to be **afraid** of."

Award-Winning Author/Illustrator

The Story Blue

Genre

Fiction

In fiction for children, animals sometimes act like people.

Look for:

- **Ways the birds in the story act like people.**
- **Ways the birds are like real birds.**

# of a Bird

by Tomek Bogacki

A little blue bird was born in the nest of a big tree. He grew fast.

"Why don't you go and learn how to fly with your brother and sister? Don't you wonder what is out there?" his mother asked.

"Oh, yes. But I am still a little bit afraid," the blue bird answered.

So while the other birds tested their wings the little blue bird sat in the nest, watching.

At night he couldn't sleep, imagining what might be out there beyond the trees.

"Mama, Mama, what is out there?" he asked.

"Nothing," she said. "Now go to sleep."

Nothing? he wondered . . . And he couldn't stop thinking about it.

The next morning the little blue bird was gone, and everyone wondered what had happened.

"Nothing, nothing, where is this nothing?" the little blue bird thought as he walked away from his nest in the big tree.

"Is nothing high, or is nothing low?
Is nothing here, or is nothing there?
What does nothing look like?"

There was no one to ask, so he kept on going.

He came upon a pool of blue water. It looked like nothing he had ever seen before, but he didn't know if this was the nothing he was looking for.

"What are you looking for?" someone asked him.

“Nothing,” he answered, surprised.
“Oh! Come with me,” said the green bird.

And the blue bird joined him.

Suddenly a flock of colorful
birds came flying by.

"What are you looking for?"
they asked.
"Nothing," the green bird
answered.
"Oh! Come with us,"
they called.

And the green bird spread
his wings and flew up.

And the little blue bird forgot that he was afraid of flying. He, too, spread his wings and flew up to join them.

And they flew high, and they flew low. They flew here, and they flew there.

"How wonderful it is to fly," the little blue bird thought.

"Where have you been? What have you seen?" asked his brother and sister when the blue bird came back home.

"What happened to make you fly so well?" asked his mother.

"Nothing," said the blue bird, happily fluttering his wings.

"Tell us, tell us all about it," said his brother and sister.

"Come with me!" said the blue bird.

And they flew high, and they flew low.

They flew here, and they flew there. They flew everywhere . . . all together.

Think and Respond

1. What was the little blue bird looking for? What does he find?
2. How does the green bird help the blue bird?
3. Why is it easier for the blue bird to fly with his new friends than alone?
4. Tell about the first time you tried to do something. Tell what you did and how you felt.
5. What lesson does the blue bird learn in the story?

Teacher Read-Aloud

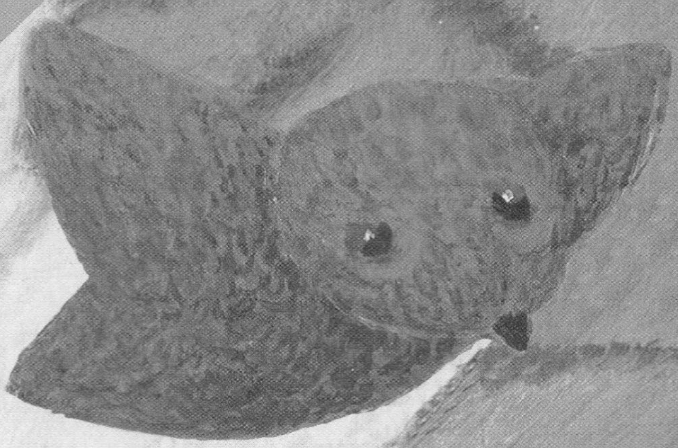

Meet the Author/Illustrator

Tomek Bogacki

Tomek Bogacki grew up in his grandparents' big house near a river in Poland. He rode his bike to the meadows at the edge of town. He also drew, painted, and wrote stories.

Now Tomek Bogacki illustrates and writes children's books. Children all over the world have enjoyed them, so he keeps making new ones.

Tomek Bogacki

Visit *The Learning Site!*
www.harcourtschool.com

Teacher Read-Aloud

▲ The Story of a Blue Bird

Making Connections

If You Could Fly

If you could fly like a bird, where would you go? What would you see from the air? Draw and write your ideas. Share your work.

Writing CONNECTION

My Flight

I flew over a park.
I saw lots of grass.
I saw a man walking his dog.

Birds and Their Nests

Science/
Technology
CONNECTION

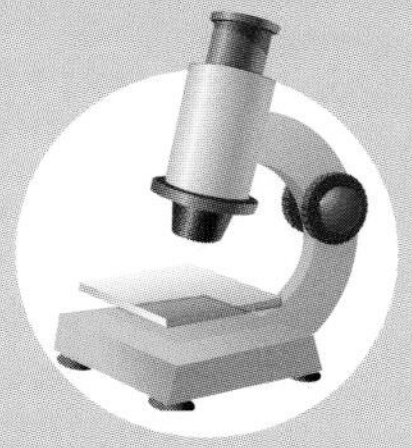

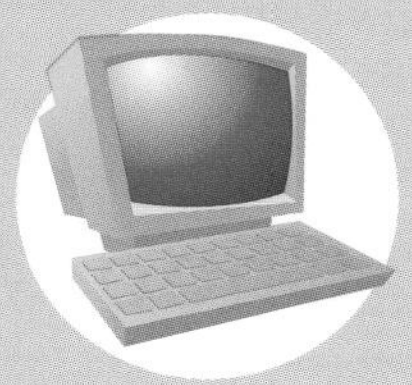

The little blue bird hatched from an egg in a nest. Find out more about birds and bird nests. Share what you learn.

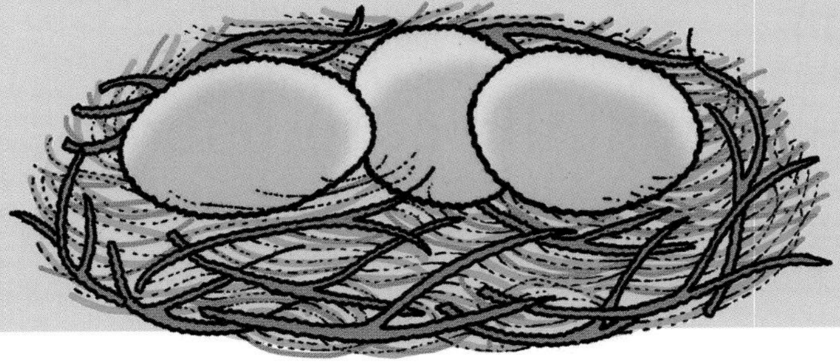

Nothing = Zero

Math
CONNECTION

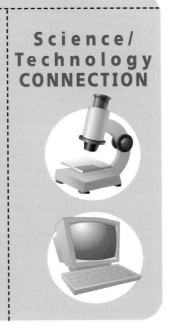

The little blue bird didn't understand what **nothing** means. Another word for **nothing** is **zero**. Draw and write a number sentence that ends with zero.

Teacher Read-Aloud

▲ The Story of a Blue Bird

Plot

Focus Skill

The main things that happen in a story make up the **plot** of that story.

Think about "The Story of a Blue Bird." What important things happen? Choose the sentence that best tells the **plot.**

1. A little bird hatches from an egg and grows fast.
2. A little bird walks to a pool of blue water.
3. A little bird is afraid at first, but at last he learns to fly.

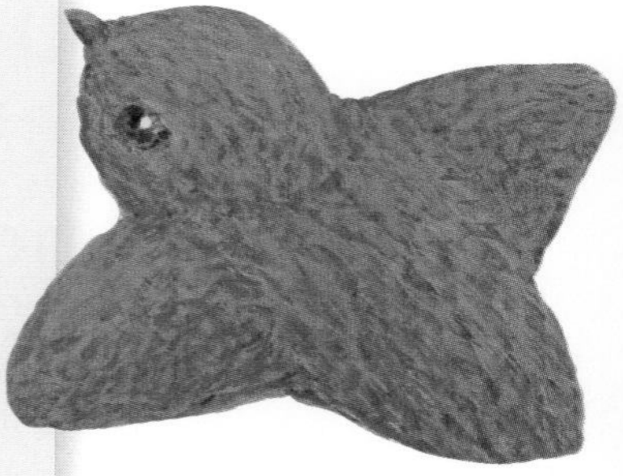

Why do you think the sentence you chose best tells the **plot** of the story?

Visit *The Learning Site!*
www.harcourtschool.com
See *Skills* and *Activities*

Test Prep
Plot

GEORGIA CRCT Tested Skill

Read this story.

Chuck at Bat

The bases were loaded. Chuck was at bat. "Crack!" went the bat. It was a home run! "We will win!" shouted Chuck's team.

I. Which sentence best tells the plot of the story?

- ○ Chuck did not want to bat.
- ○ Chuck shouted, "We will win!"
- ○ Chuck helped his team win.

Tip

Think about the important things that happen. Then read each answer choice carefully.

▲ Frog and Toad All Year

Word Power

Words to Remember

caught

cold

hurried

near

son

sure

It was a very **cold** day.
Frog was standing **near** his father.
"**Son**, it's going to snow," said his father.
"Let's make **sure** that we don't get **caught** in the storm."
Frog and his father **hurried** home.

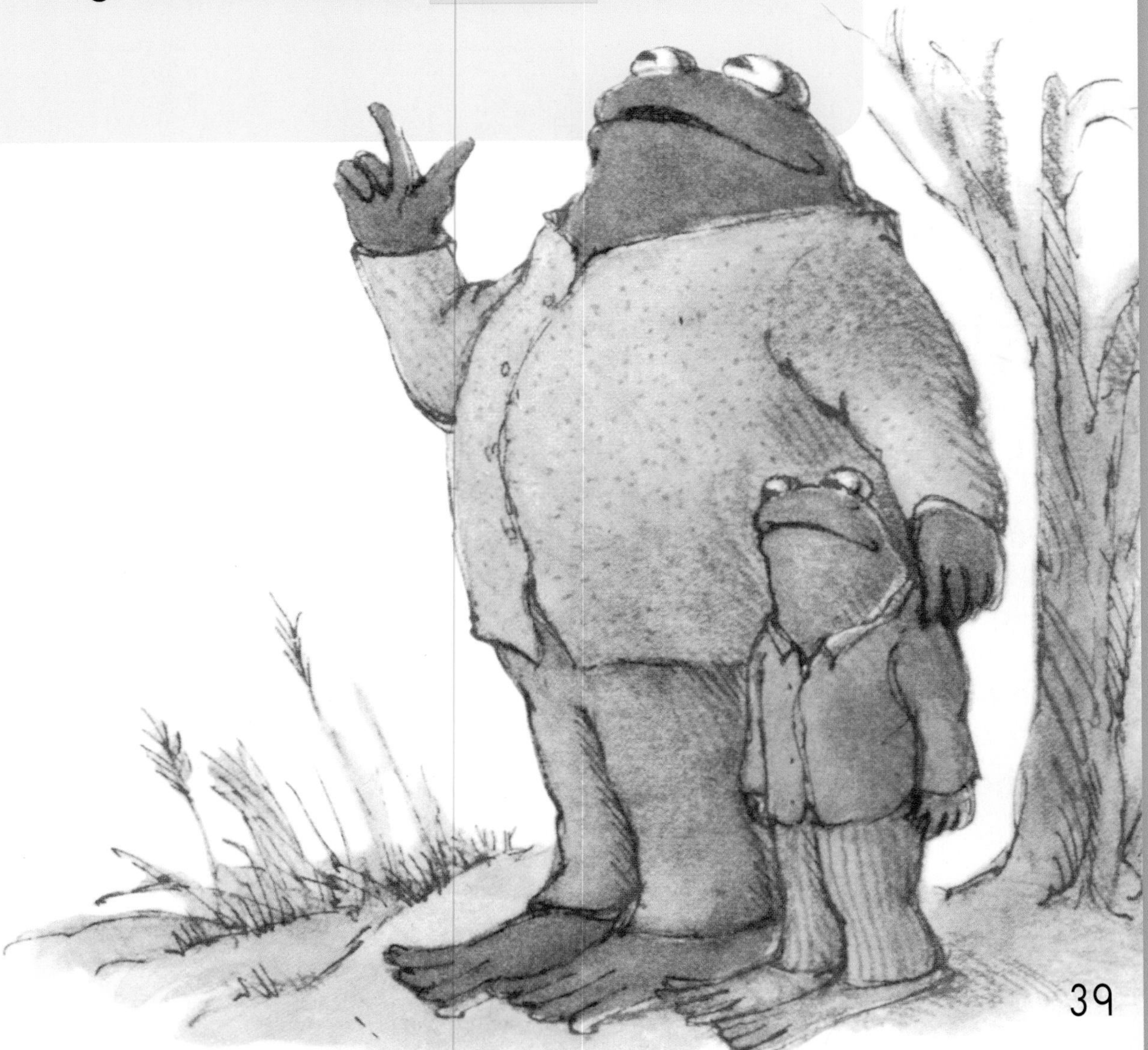

Genre

Fiction

Sometimes in fiction there is a "story within a story."

Look for:

- **the parts of the story that are happening in the story present— or now.**
- **the story that one character tells about the past.**

FROG AND TOAD ALL YEAR

by Arnold Lobel

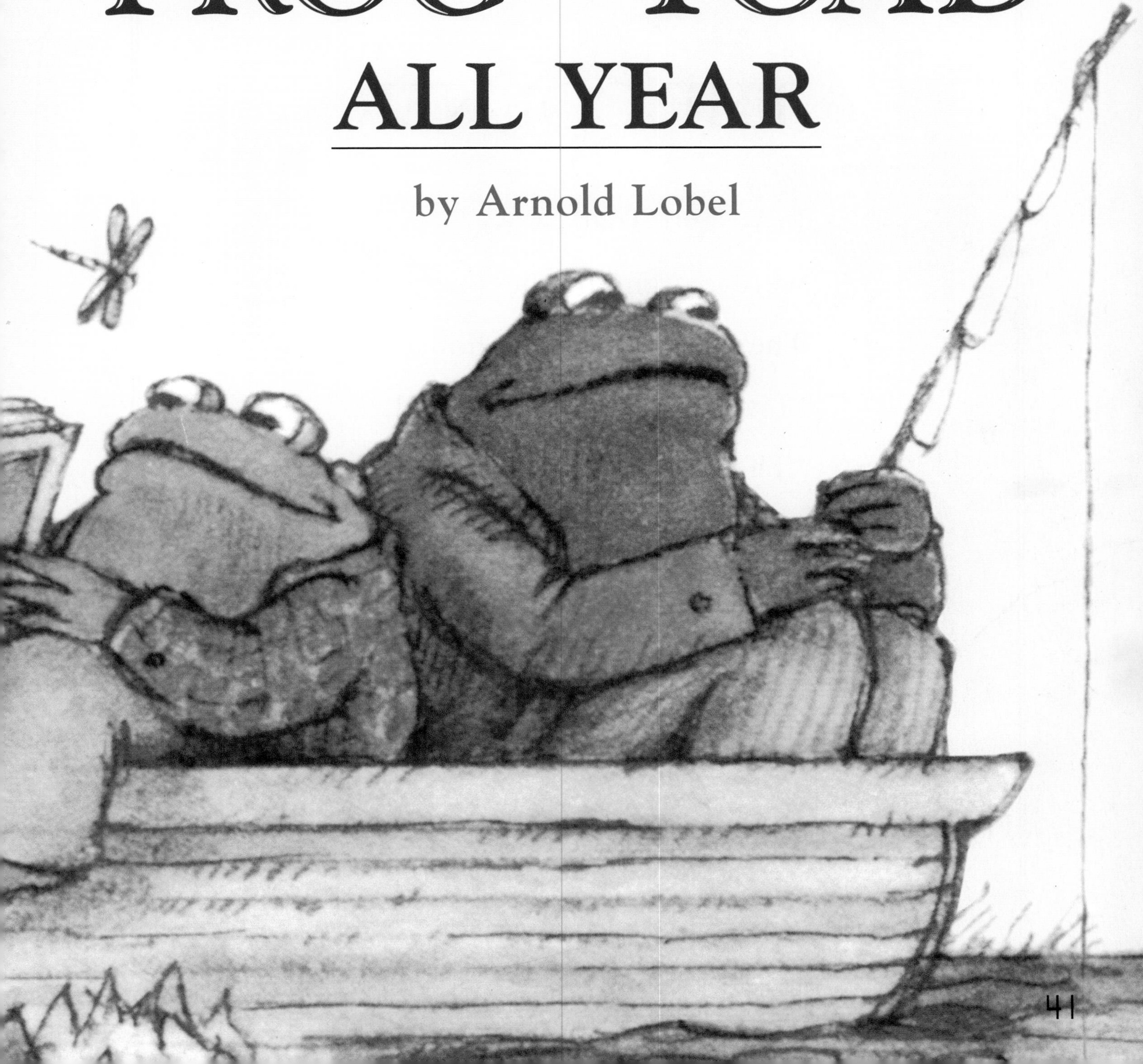

THE CORNER

Frog and Toad
were caught in the rain.
They ran to Frog's house.
"I am all wet," said Toad.
"The day is spoiled."
"Have some tea and cake,"
said Frog. "The rain will stop.
If you stand near the stove,
your clothes will soon be dry.

I will tell you a story
while we are waiting," said Frog.
"Oh good," said Toad.

"When I was small,
not much bigger
than a pollywog," said Frog,
"my father said to me,
'Son, this is a cold, gray day
but spring
is just around the corner.'

I wanted spring to come.
I went out
to find that corner.
I walked down a path in the woods
until I came to a corner.
I went around the corner
to see if spring
was on the other side."

"And was it?" asked Toad.

"No," said Frog.

"There was only a pine tree,

three pebbles

and some dry grass.

I walked
in the meadow.
Soon I came to
another corner.
I went around the corner
to see if spring was there."
"Did you find it?" asked Toad.

"No," said Frog.
"There was only
an old worm
asleep on a
tree stump."

"I walked along the river
until I came to
another corner.
I went around the corner
to look for spring."
"Was it there?" asked Toad.

"No," said Frog.
"There was only
some wet mud
and a lizard who was chasing
his tail."
"You must have been tired,"
said Toad.
"I was tired," said Frog,
"and it started
to rain."

"I went back home.

When I got there," said Frog,

"I found another corner.

It was the corner of my house."

"Did you go around it?"

asked Toad.

"I went around that corner, too,"

said Frog.

"What did you see?"

asked Toad.

"I saw the sun coming out,"
said Frog. "I saw birds
sitting and singing in a tree.
I saw my mother and father
working in their garden.
I saw flowers in the garden."

"You found it!" cried Toad.

"Yes," said Frog.

"I was very happy.

I had found the corner

that spring was just around."

"Look, Frog," said Toad.

"You were right.

The rain has stopped."

Frog and Toad hurried outside.

They ran around the corner
of Frog's house
to make sure
that spring had come again.

Think and Respond

1. What does Frog do to find spring?
2. What signs of spring does Frog find?
3. How does Frog's story help Toad feel better?
4. Tell about a time when a friend did something that made you feel better.
5. What did you like most about this story? Tell why.

Teacher Read-Aloud

ABOUT THE AUTHOR/ILLUSTRATOR

ARNOLD LOBEL

Arnold Lobel was both a writer and an illustrator of books for children. Frog and Toad are two of the many wonderful characters he created. He got the idea to write about frogs and toads while sitting on his front porch. He thought about frogs and toads, which look alike but are very different. Then he began writing about the characters we know today.

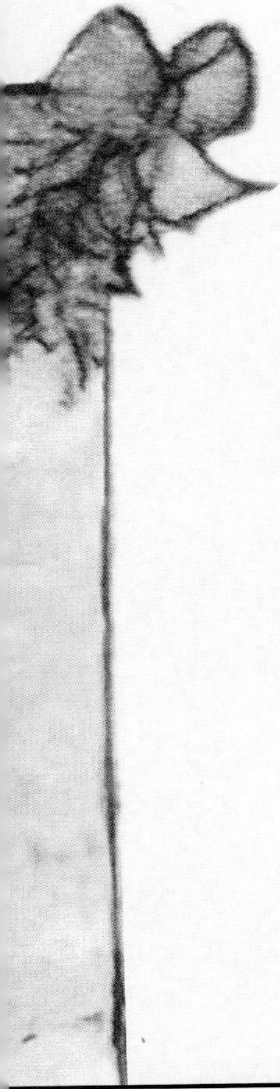

Visit *The Learning Site!*
www.harcourtschool.com

Teacher Read-Aloud
Magazine Article

Frogs in Trees?

by Mark Warner

What do you think of when you think of frogs? Things that hop, right? Well how about things that *climb?* Some frogs climb bushes and trees. These frogs are called *tree frogs.*

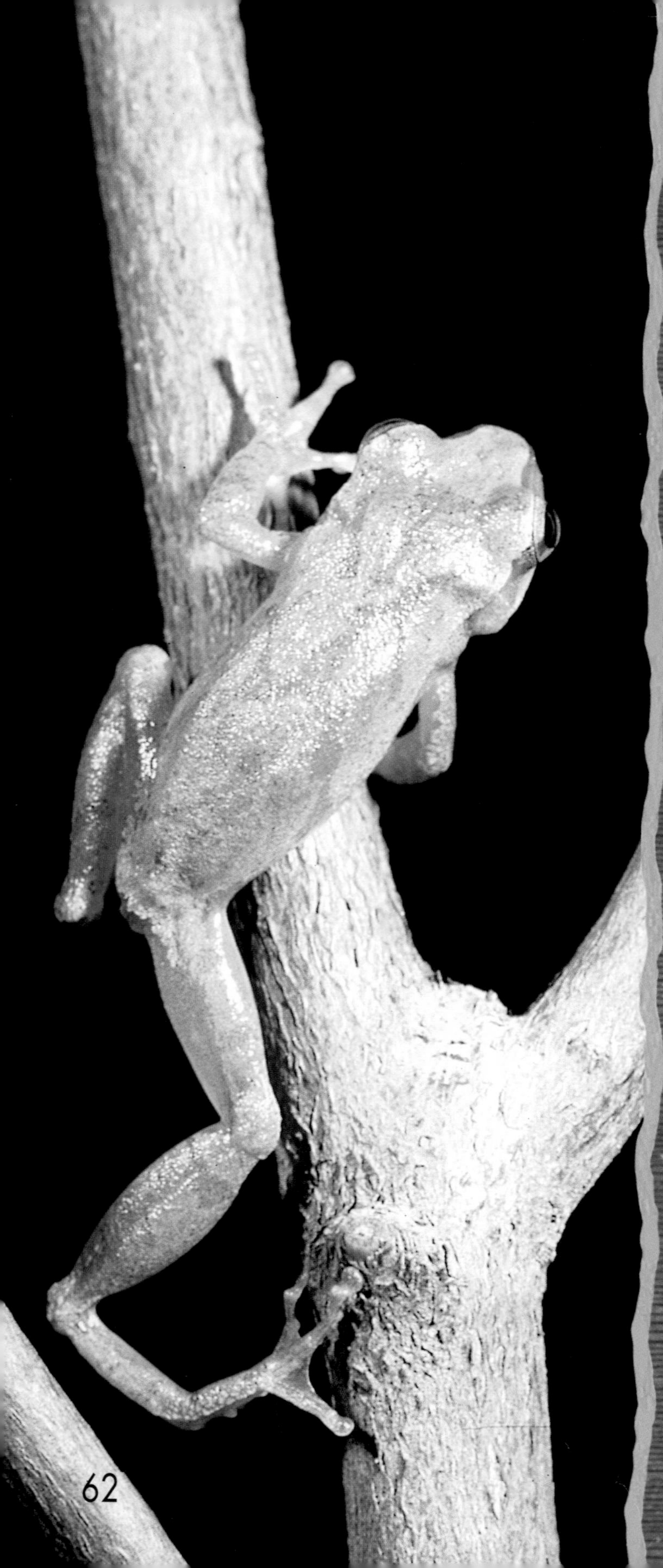

The tree frogs climb trees to look for food. The big eyes on top of their heads make it easy for them to see insects they want to eat. The big eyes also help the tree frogs see bigger animals that might want to eat them!

◀ Tree frogs have sticky pads on the tips of their toes. These pads help them hold on to trees as they climb.

Most tree frogs are small. Being small makes it easier to climb trees. This full-grown tree frog can easily fit on a person's thumb. ►

Tree frogs are good at hiding. Some even change color to help them hide. This gray tree frog blends in with the tree bark. Can you see the frog? ►

Teacher Read-Aloud

▲ Frog and Toad All Year

Making Connections

Around the Corner

Frog went around a lot of corners before he found what he was looking for! What would you like to find "just around the corner"? Finish these sentences.

I went around the corner.
There I found _____.

Draw a picture to go with what you write.

Writing CONNECTION

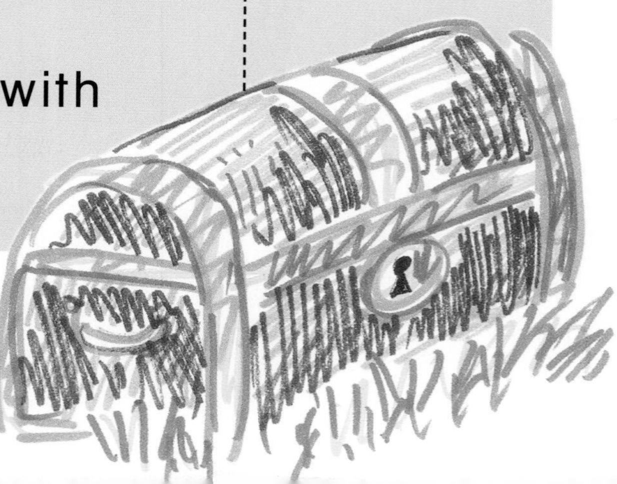

A Frog's Life

You have learned some things about real frogs. Find out something else about frogs. Share what you learn.

Science/ Technology CONNECTION

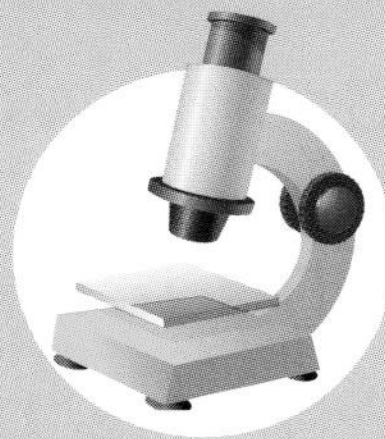

Jump and Measure

Jump like a frog as far as you can. Have two friends measure with yarn how far you jumped. Take turns. Then compare pieces of yarn. Who jumped the farthest?

Math CONNECTION

Teacher Read-Aloud

▲ Frog and Toad All Year

Words with *ai* and *ay*

Phonics Skill

You know the long sound of **a** spelled a-e in words like **cake** and **game.**

The letters **ai** and **ay** can also stand for the long sound of **a**. Here are some words from "Frog and Toad All Year."

rain	**waiting**	**tail**
gray	**day**	

Put these groups of letters in order to make two words with the long sound of **a**.

y t s a	**i a n m**

You may want to use your Word Builder.

Test Prep

Long Vowel: /ā/ *ai, ay*

GEORGIA CRCT Tested Skill

1. Choose a word that names the picture.

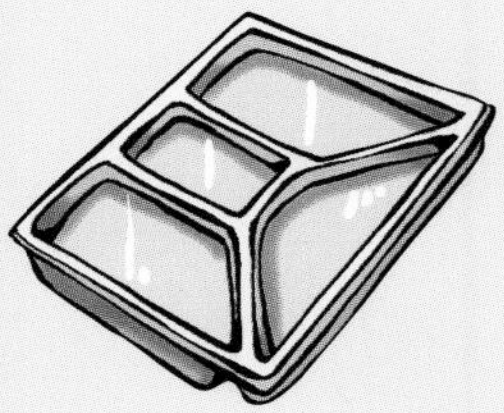

train ○ tape ○ tray ○

2. Choose a word that names the picture.

sale ○ snail ○ snack ○

Tip

Look at the words carefully. Read each word from beginning to end.

▲ Fishing Bears

Word Power

Words to Remember

both

during

ready

Both of these bears need to eat now.
They have to get **ready** for winter.
They will sleep a lot **during** the winter.

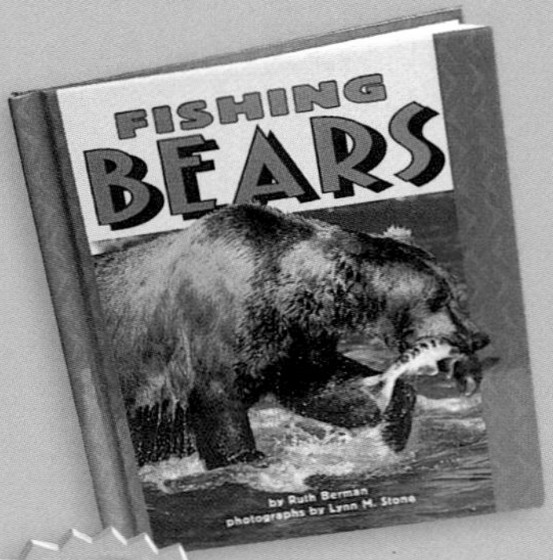

Award-Winning Author

Genre

Nonfiction

Some nonfiction pieces use photographs to give information.

Look for:

- **Ways the photographs add information.**
- **Facts about bears that may be new to you.**

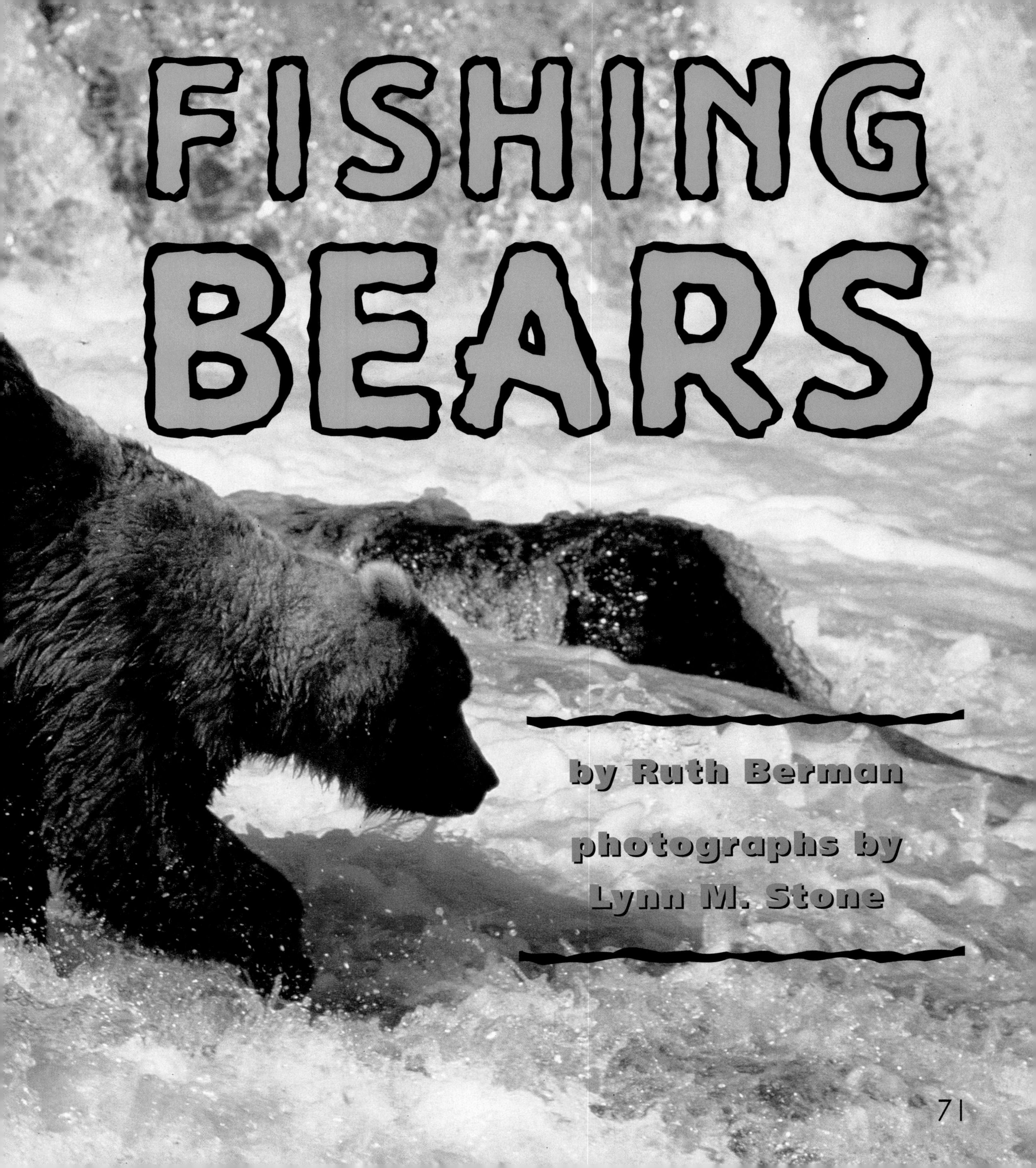

FISHING BEARS

by Ruth Berman

photographs by Lynn M. Stone

These are brown bear tracks. How many toe marks can you count?

This is an Alaskan brown bear.
Alaskan brown bears live near water.

They have small ears, small eyes, and a big long nose.

Bears can stand up on their hind legs.

This mother bear stands to smell the air for food and for enemies.

Mother bears usually have twins or triplets.

Baby bears are called cubs.

Cubs stay with their mothers for one to three years.

This cub is napping on Mom!

These cubs are playing.

Brown bears eat both plants and animals.

Most furry animals walk on their toes.

Bears walk with their feet
flat on the ground.

These bears are walking on a trail.

The trail ends at a river. Brown bears look for fish in rivers.

Look! These bears are fighting over a good fishing spot.

The bigger bear wins. It is about to catch a salmon!

What do you think this bear is doing?

It is fishing for salmon under the water.

These bears are pouncing on salmon.

Can you find a mother and her cubs in this picture?

The mother is keeping her cubs safe from a male bear.

This small bear is trying to sneak some food!

Alaskan brown bears also eat clams.

Bears have to dig for clams.

Alaskan brown bears get ready for winter by eating a lot.

Eating a lot makes them fat.

Why do bears need to get fat?

Fat keeps them warm and healthy during the winter.

Brown bears stay in dens for most of the winter. A brown bear is hibernating in this cozy den.

When bears hibernate, they are in a deep sleep.

In the spring, bears leave their dens to look for food.

Then bears eat and eat.

They will be fat again by next winter.

Fishing is hard work!
It is time to rest.

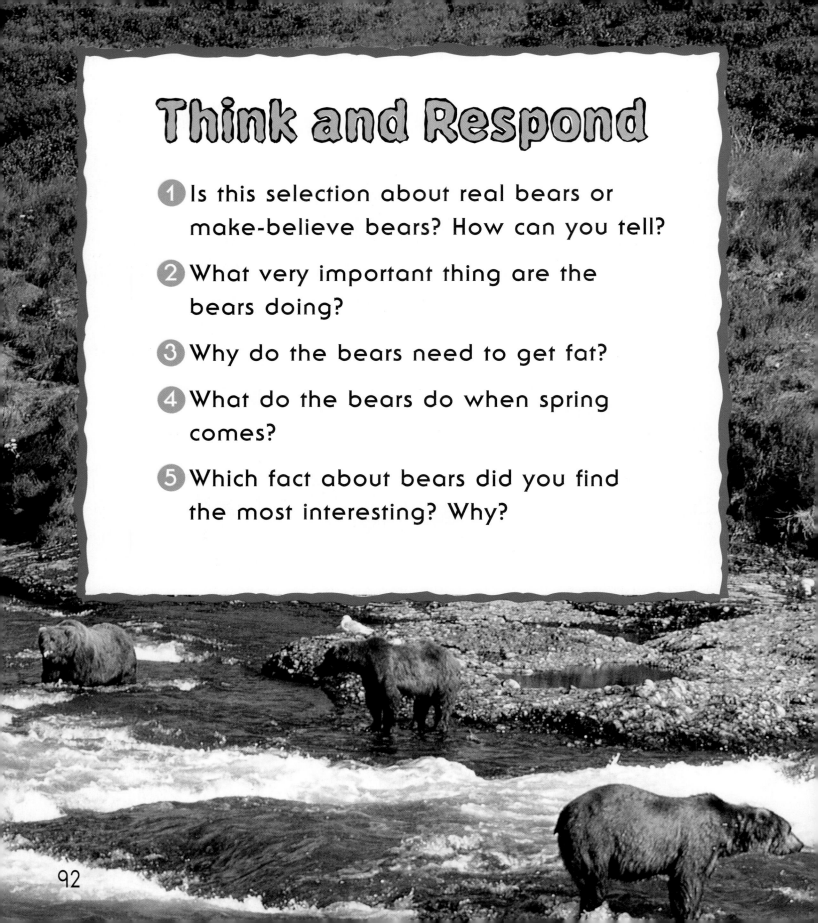

Think and Respond

1. Is this selection about real bears or make-believe bears? How can you tell?
2. What very important thing are the bears doing?
3. Why do the bears need to get fat?
4. What do the bears do when spring comes?
5. Which fact about bears did you find the most interesting? Why?

Meet the Author

Ruth Berman

Ruth Berman lives in California with her husband, her daughter, two dogs, and a cat. She likes writing for children. She says, "I hope my books teach children to love and respect animals."

Meet the Photographer

Lynn M. Stone

Lynn M. Stone took the pictures for *Fishing Bears* in a bear sanctuary in Alaska. Animals are protected there. Only a few people enter the sanctuary each year. "I felt like I had won a prize when I was picked to go into the sanctuary," says Mr. Stone.

Teacher Read-Aloud

▲ Fishing Bears

Making Connections

Life in Alaska

Alaskan bears sleep during the long, cold winter. What do people who live in Alaska do to keep safe and warm in winter? Use the Internet to find out. Share one thing you learn.

Social Studies/ Technology CONNECTION

How Many Babies?

Math CONNECTION

Most Alaskan mother bears have twins or triplets. If the mother bear has triplets, how many babies does she have? Make a chart of words like **twins** and **triplets**. Draw to show how many baby animals each word means.

twins=  2

triplets=

quadruplets=

quintuplets =

Bear Captions

Writing CONNECTION

Choose a picture that you like from the story. Write a sentence or two to go with it. Say something different than what the author said. Write something silly if you like!

Wake up, little bear! It's time to go fishing.

Teacher Read-Aloud

▲ Fishing Bears

Main Idea

Focus Skill

The **main idea** of a nonfiction piece is what that piece is mostly about. You read facts about bears in "Fishing Bears." Read these sentences. Which tells the **main idea**?

1. **Alaskan brown bears have small ears and a big, long nose.**
2. **Bears fight over good fishing spots.**
3. **Alaskan brown bears must eat a lot before they sleep in winter.**

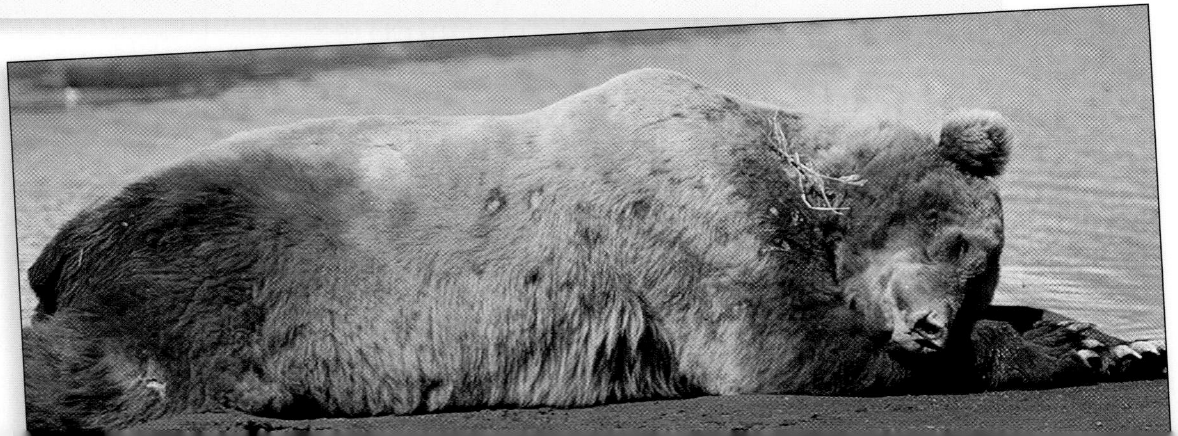

Visit *The Learning Site!*
www.harcourtschool.com
See *Skills* and *Activities*

Test Prep
Main Idea

GEORGIA CRCT Tested Skill

Fish have fins to help them swim. Most fish have strong tail fins. They swing their tail fins to swim fast. Other fins help fish make turns.

1. Which sentence tells the main idea?

- ○ Fish swing their tail fins.
- ○ Fish use fins to swim.
- ○ Fish use fins to make turns.

Tip

Read the sentences carefully. Which sentence tells what the whole piece is mostly about?

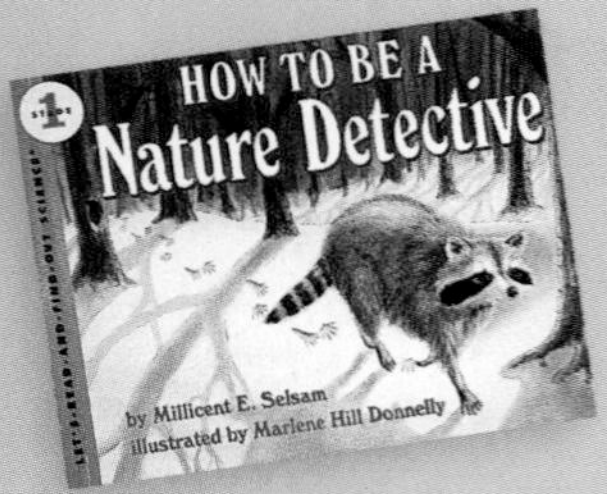

▲ How to Be a Nature Detective

Word Power

Words to Remember

clues

detective

floor

nature

piece

pulls

A **detective** looks for **clues**.
A **nature detective** looks for **clues**, too. They may be tracks in mud, in sand, or even on a **floor**. A **nature detective** sometimes **pulls** a stick or a **piece** of string out of a nest. Find out how to be a **nature detective**!

Award-Winning Author

Genre

Nonfiction

There are many ways an author can give information in nonfiction.

Look for:

- **Ways the author lets you figure out answers to questions.**
- **Ideas the author gives about ways to learn from nature.**

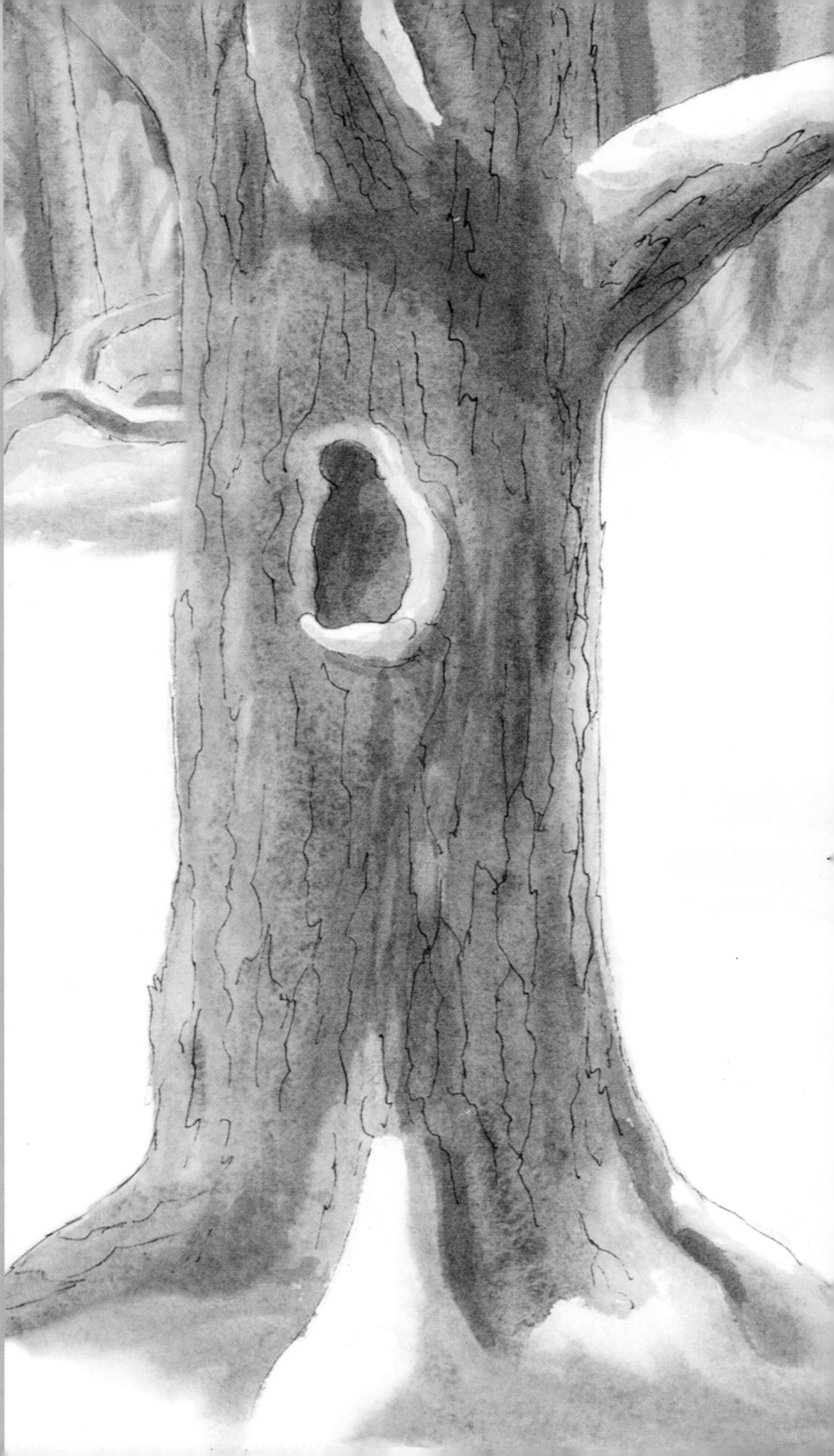

How to Be a Nature Detective

by Millicent E. Selsam
illustrated by Marlene Hill Donnelly

"What happened?" a detective says.
"Who was here?
"Where did he go?"
A detective has many ways to find out.

One way is to look for the marks someone or something has made—fingerprints, footprints, the tracks made by bike tires.

Sometimes a detective finds a hair, a button, a piece of torn clothing. All these things are clues. They help a detective answer these questions: What happened? Who was here? Where did he go?

You can be a detective too, a special kind of detective—a nature detective.

Nature detectives find tracks and clues that answer these questions: What animal walked here? Where did it go? What did it do? What did it eat?

Where does a nature detective look for clues? Almost anywhere—in a backyard, in the woods, in a city park.

You can find tracks in many places—in mud, in snow, in sand, in dust, even on the sidewalk or on the floor. Wet feet or wet muddy paws can make tracks anywhere.

Here is a problem for a nature detective:

Here is a cat.

Here is a dog.

Here is a dish for the cat.

Here is a dish for the dog.

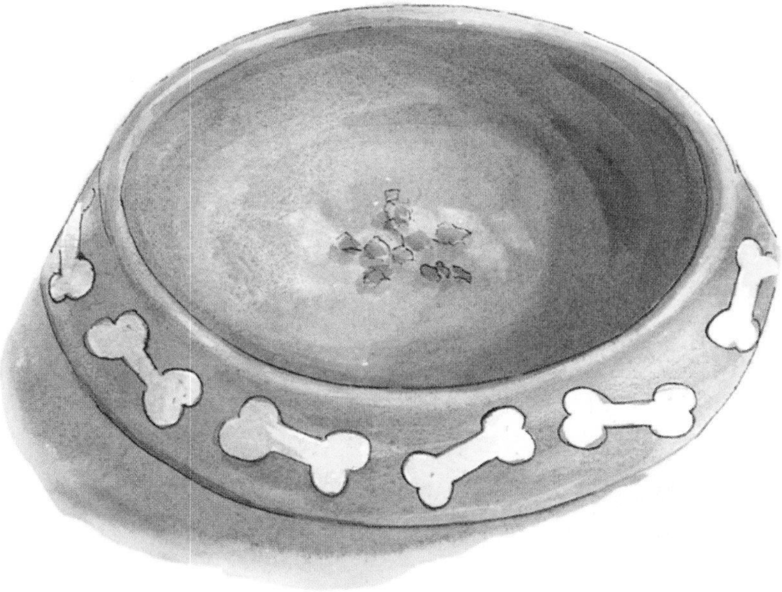

The cat's dish had milk in it. The dog's dish had meat in it. Who drank the milk? Who ate the meat?

Look at the tracks and see.

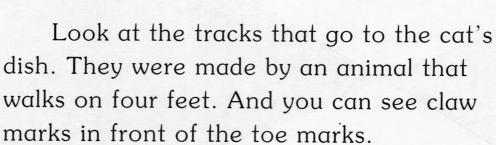

Look at the tracks that go to the cat's dish. They were made by an animal that walks on four feet. And you can see claw marks in front of the toe marks.

A cat has four feet and sharp claws. But so does a dog.

Who went to the cat's dish?

We still don't know.

Let's look for more clues.

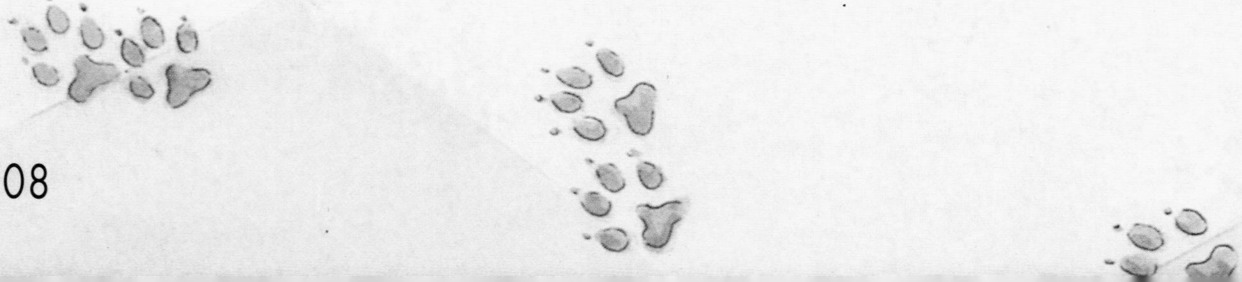

No claw marks!

Now look at the other tracks—the tracks that go to the dog's dish.

Did you ever watch a cat walk?

A cat walks on four feet. But the tracks of his hind feet fall exactly on the tracks of his front feet. So his footprints are one behind the other, in one line. They look like the footprints of an animal with only two feet. A cat pulls his claws in when he walks. So he does not leave claw marks.

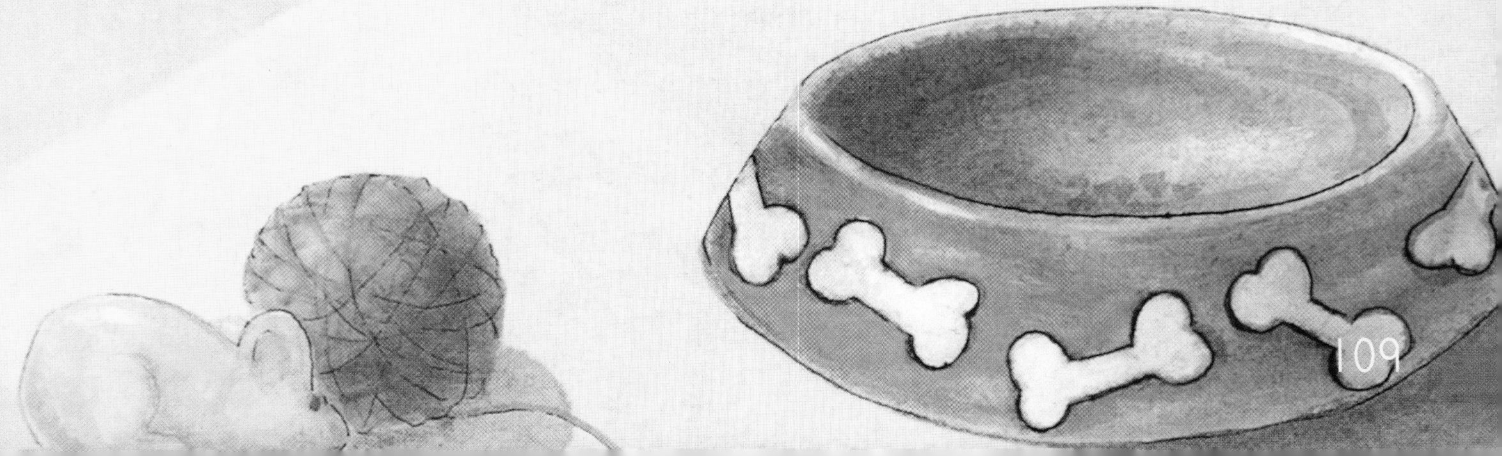

Now do you know who drank the milk? (THE DOG!)
Now do you know who ate the dog food? (THE CAT!)

A nature detective can find many clues on a sandy beach.

When you walk on the beach in the morning, look for sea gull tracks. They can tell you which way the wind was blowing when the gulls were there.

Like airplanes, sea gulls take off facing into the wind. First the gulls must run along the sand to get up speed for takeoff. As they run, their toes dig deeper into the sand.

Here all the gull toe tracks are in a line facing east. So you know that the wind came from the east.

Tracks are good clues for a nature detective. But there are other clues, too.

Who lives here?
Who ate here?

A nature detective learns to look and listen—and smell. She can find clues in a backyard, in the woods, or in a city park.

Who made that smell?

Think and Respond

1. How is a nature detective like other detectives?
2. Which animal tracks do the detectives in the story look at?
3. What surprise does the author give the reader about the dog and the cat?
4. What are some good places to find nature clues?
5. Which animals would you like to find out more about?

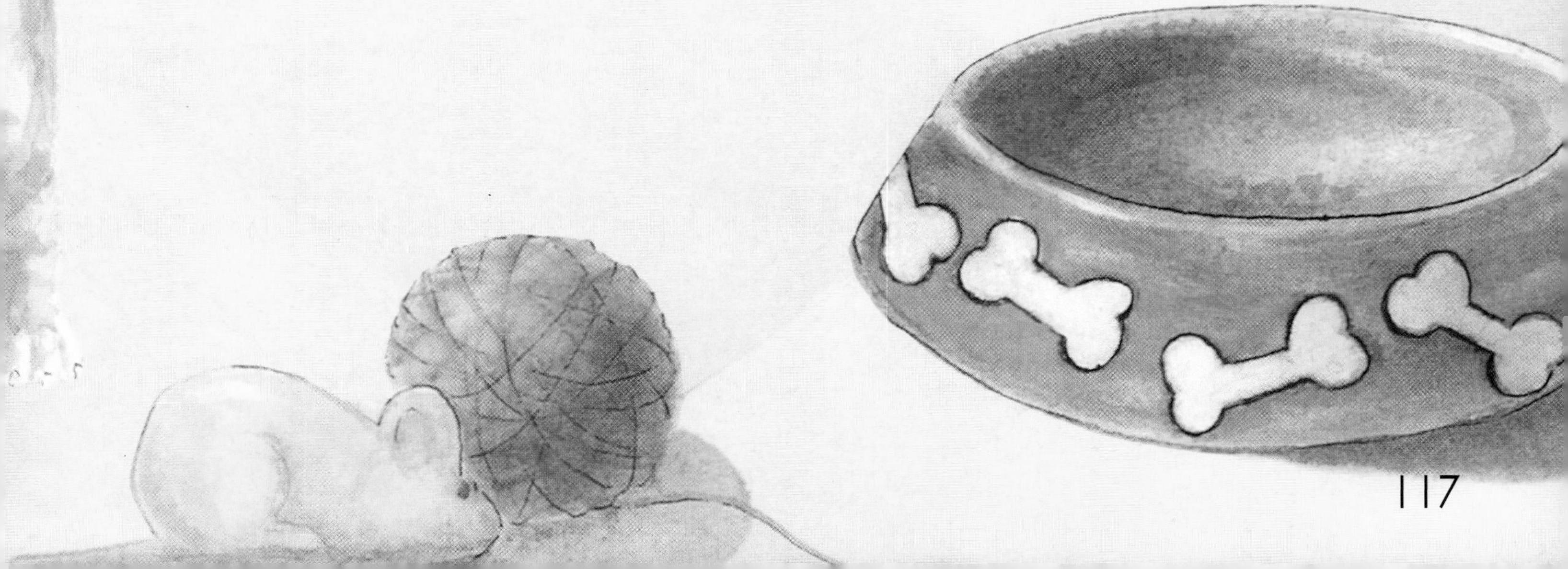

About the Author

Millicent E. Selsam

Millicent Selsam always liked science and nature. She said, "I love to investigate everything." Before writing each book, she would read about the subject she wanted to share with children. Millicent Selsam wrote more than 130 books! She won many, many awards for her work. Her books have helped children learn to look at their world in a new way.

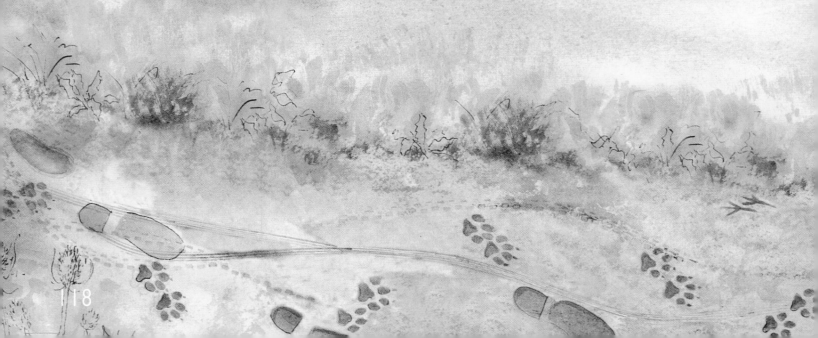

Meet the Illustrator

Marlene Hill Donnelly

Marlene Hill Donnelly draws things found in nature. Her work has been shown in zoos and aquariums across the United States. How did her pictures help you see nature in a new way?

Teacher Read-Aloud

▲ How to Be a Nature Detective

Making Connections

Nature Detective Walk

With your teacher, walk around your school or in a park. Look for clues that tell you which animals live there. Make a class list of your findings.

Science CONNECTION

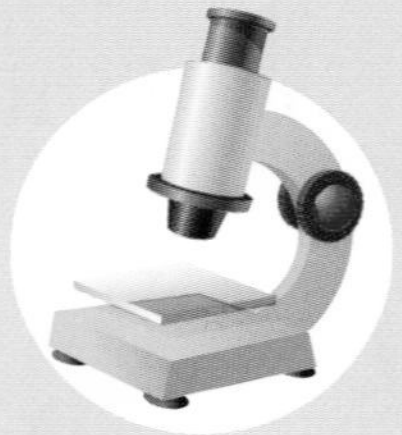

Clues in Nature

animal tracks
empty nests
shells

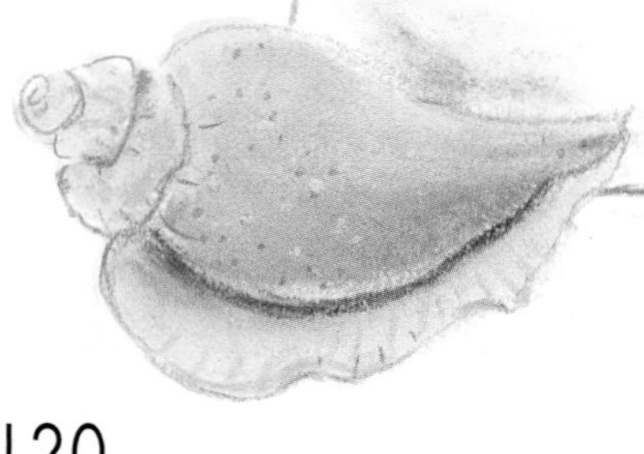

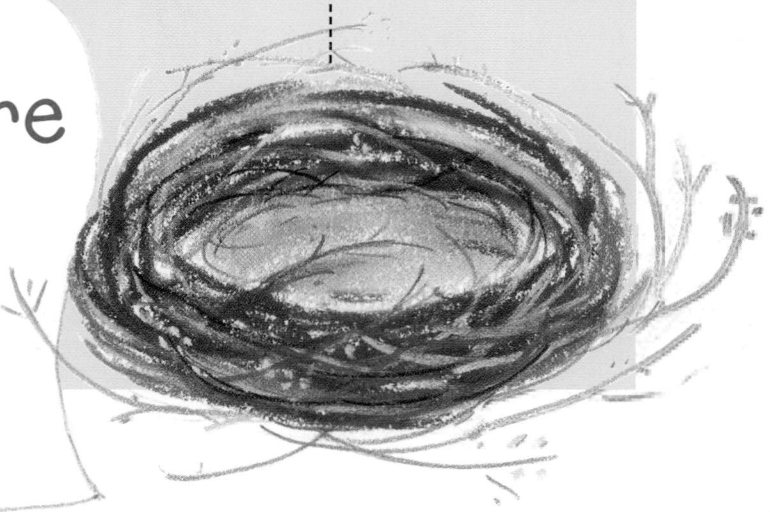

Just In!

Writing CONNECTION

Write a TV news story for NDN, the Nature Detective Network. Tell about a nature clue you have found—or one you wish you had found!

Elephant tracks were seen in the schoolyard today!

Poster Paws

Art CONNECTION

Find out how other animal tracks look. Draw a set of tracks and write the animal's name under them. Add your work to a class poster.

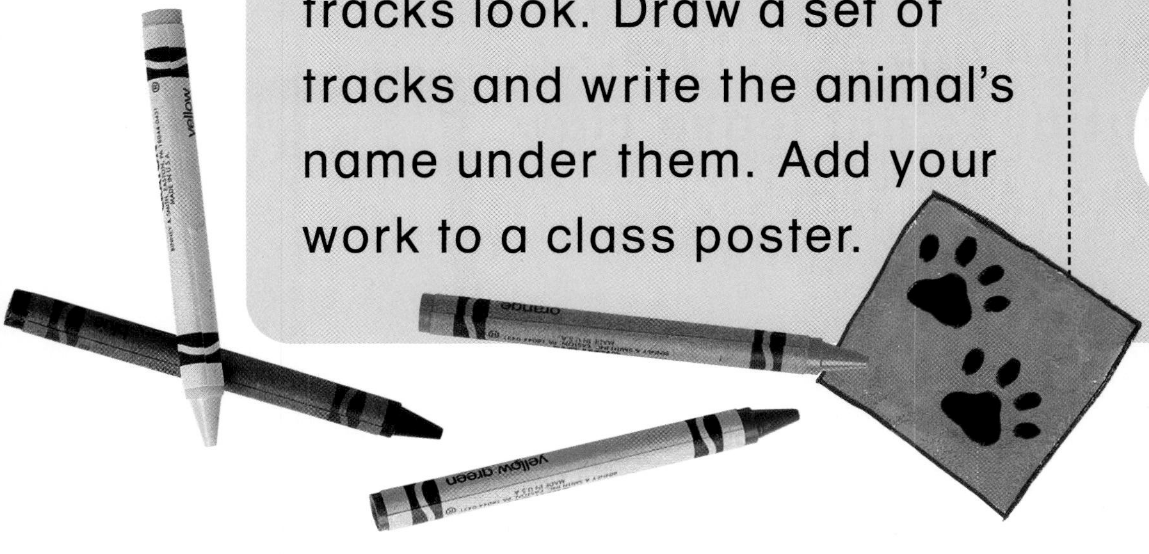

Teacher Read-Aloud

▲ How to Be a Nature Detective

Main Idea

Focus Skill

You have learned that the **main idea** of a nonfiction piece is what that piece is mostly about. Think about "How to Be a Nature Detective." Which sentence tells the main idea?

1. A nature detective can find many clues on a sandy beach.
2. A nature detective uses sight, smell, and hearing to find clues about things in nature.
3. A cat does not leave claw marks in its tracks.

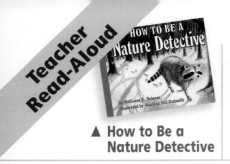

Visit *The Learning Site!*
www.harcourtschool.com
See *Skills* and *Activities*

Test Prep

Main Idea

GEORGIA CRCT Tested Skill

Fox tracks are like dog tracks in some ways and cat tracks in other ways. Fox tracks are in one line like cat tracks. They show claw marks like dog tracks.

1. Which sentence tells the main idea?

- ○ Fox tracks show claw marks.
- ○ Fox tracks are in one line.
- ○ Fox tracks are like both dog tracks and cat tracks.

Tip

Read the sentences carefully. Which sentence tells what the whole story is about?

▲ The Puddle

Word Power

Words to Remember

angry

okay

nearly

sorry

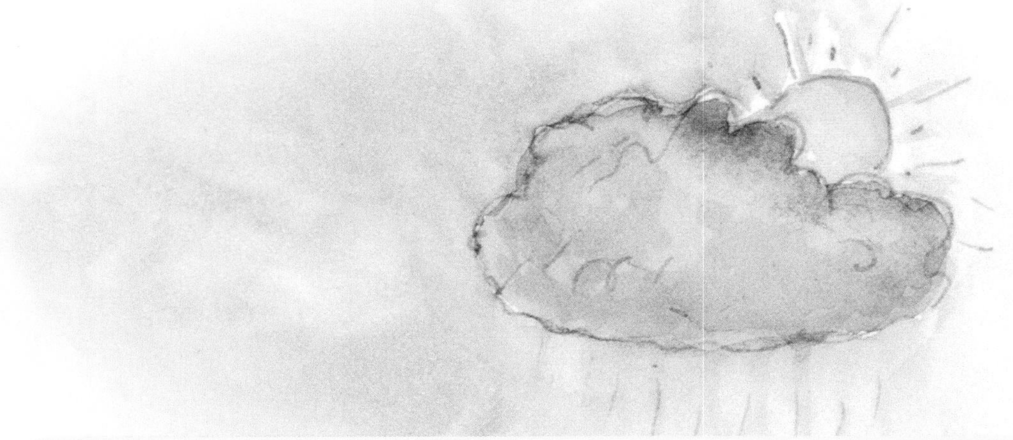

I'm feeling **angry**. That frog **nearly** sank my boat! He said he was **sorry**. I said it was **okay**. I will not let him take my boat again.

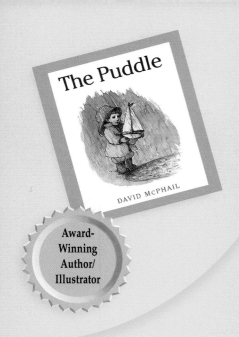

Award-Winning Author/Illustrator

Genre

Fiction

In fiction, there can be a mix of realistic and make-believe parts.

Look for:

- **Ways the story is like real life.**
- **Things that could not happen in real life.**

The

by David McPhail

Puddle

It was a rainy day.

I asked my mom if I
could go out and sail
my boat in the puddles.
She said, "**Okay**, but *you*
stay out of the puddles."

I got dressed in
my rain boots and
coat, and went to
sail my boat in
the largest puddle
I could find.

A frog came along and
sat down beside me.
"Nice boat," he said.

Then he jumped onto my boat and sailed away. “Come back!” I called, but he wouldn’t listen.

A turtle floated by.
"Teatime," said the turtle. "Care to join me?"
"I can't," I said. "I need to get my boat back.
Besides, I'm not allowed to go in puddles."

But the frog steered my boat right into the turtle. CRASH!
The frog laughed. He thought it was funny.

The turtle didn't think it was funny at all.
She was **angry**.

Then an alligator offered to help.
"Want me to get your boat back
for you?" he asked.
"Really? That would be *great*!" I said.

So the alligator swam out to take
my boat away from the frog.
He did.

But the boat looked different
than it did before.
"**Sorry**," he said.
"Don't worry about it,"
I told him.

Next, a pig wanted to
swim in the puddle.

He took a running start,
jumped in, and splashed me.
"My mom's not gonna like this!"
I yelled to the pig.

Before long, a thirsty elephant
showed up.

She drank . . .
and drank . . .

. . . until the puddle
was **nearly** gone.

The other animals were
upset with the elephant.
"Put back the water!"
they shouted.

So she did.

She left, and when the sun started to come out, the other animals left, too.

Then the sun dried up
the rest of the puddle.
I took my boat home.

When I got there, my mom had a hot bath waiting for me.

"Can I bring my boat?" I asked her.

"Of course," she said.

And I did.

Think and Respond

1. What is your favorite part of the story? Tell why.
2. What happens when the boy tries to sail his boat in the puddle?
3. How does the boy get his boat back?
4. What would you do if you could understand an animal talking to you?
5. How does the author mix the real and the make-believe parts of the story?

Teacher Read-Aloud

Meet the Author/Illustrator

David McPhail

David McPhail grew up by the sea. He played in the woods and fields near his house. That is where he first got interested in animals. He likes to put animal characters in his stories.

He also likes to tell two stories in his books. He tells one in words and one in the illustrations. He believes that "each day is an adventure and each book is a new beginning."

David McPhail

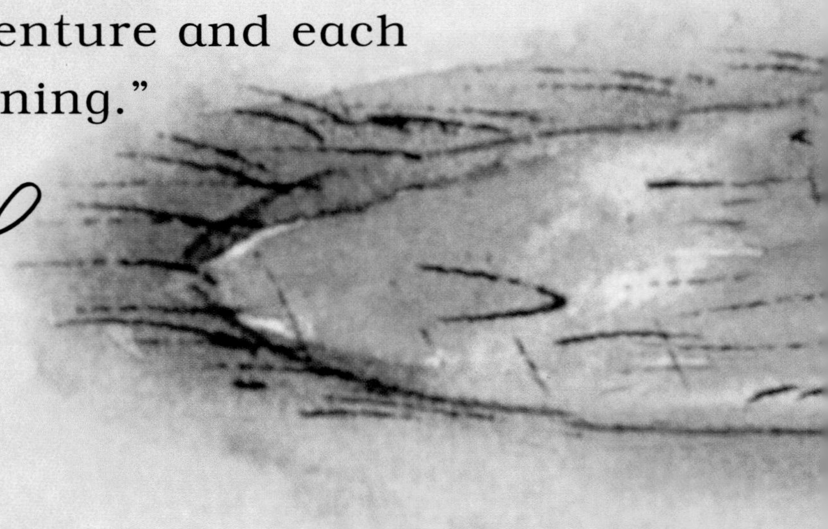

Visit *The Learning Site!*
www.harcourtschool.com

Teacher Read-Aloud
Poem

Time to Play

Mama says to play outside.
Wish I had a bike to ride.
I'll fly to the moon instead.
Steer the rocket in my head.
I'll pretend to find a star
no one else has seen so far.
Then I'll name it after me—
    Africa Lawanda Lee!
But for now I'll grab some chalk,
play hopscotch out on the walk.

by Nikki Grimes
illustrated by Floyd Cooper

Teacher Read-Aloud

▲ The Puddle

Making Connections

An Alligator Friend

The alligator was a real friend to the boy. Think about something else the alligator and the boy could do together. Write about it.

Writing CONNECTION

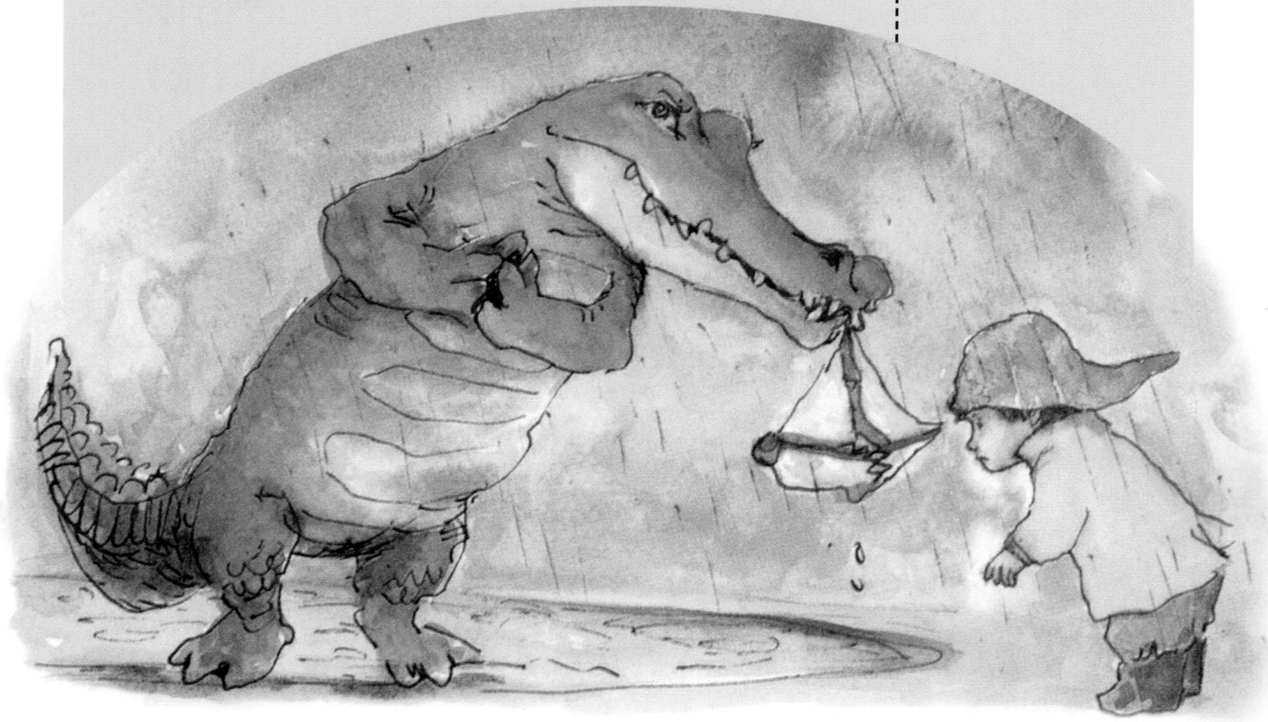

Inside, Outside

The boy in *The Puddle* played outside. Playing inside can be fun, too. Draw and write about your favorite things to do both inside and outside.

Art CONNECTION

Sing a Puddle Song

Sing this song with classmates. Make up movements to go with it.

Music CONNECTION

They'll be coming 'round the puddle when they come . . .
They'll be coming 'round the puddle when they come . . .
They'll be coming 'round the puddle.
They'll be coming 'round the puddle.
They'll be coming 'round the puddle when they come.

Teacher Read-Aloud

▲ The Puddle

Plot

Focus Skill

The **plot** of a story is what happens in that story. Think about the story "The Puddle." What happens in "The Puddle?" Choose the sentence that tells the **plot**.

1. **A frog takes a boy's boat and sails away.**
2. **A boy plays with an alligator.**
3. **A boy plays with animals in a puddle and goes home when the puddle dries up.**

Which sentence did you choose? Tell why.

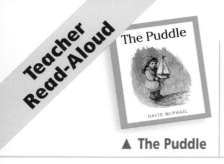

Visit *The Learning Site!*
www.harcourtschool.com
See *Skills* and *Activities*

Test Prep
Plot

GEORGIA CRCT Tested Skill

Sally had lost her Math book. At last she found it, but now she was late! She ran to the bus stop. Just then the bus came. The bus was late, too!

1. Which sentence tells the plot of the story?

- ○ Sally can't find a book at home.
- ○ Sally is late, but the school bus is late, too.
- ○ Sally runs to catch her bus.

Tip

Think of what the whole story is about. Then decide which sentence tells about the whole story.

▲ Poppleton Everyday

Word Power

Words to Remember

boy

brought

few

head

read

That pig is no longer a **boy**, but he's acting like one!

I **brought** him a book.

He **read** a **few** pages.

I even **brought** him crackers.

Look at him now! He is lying on his **head**.

What is he doing?

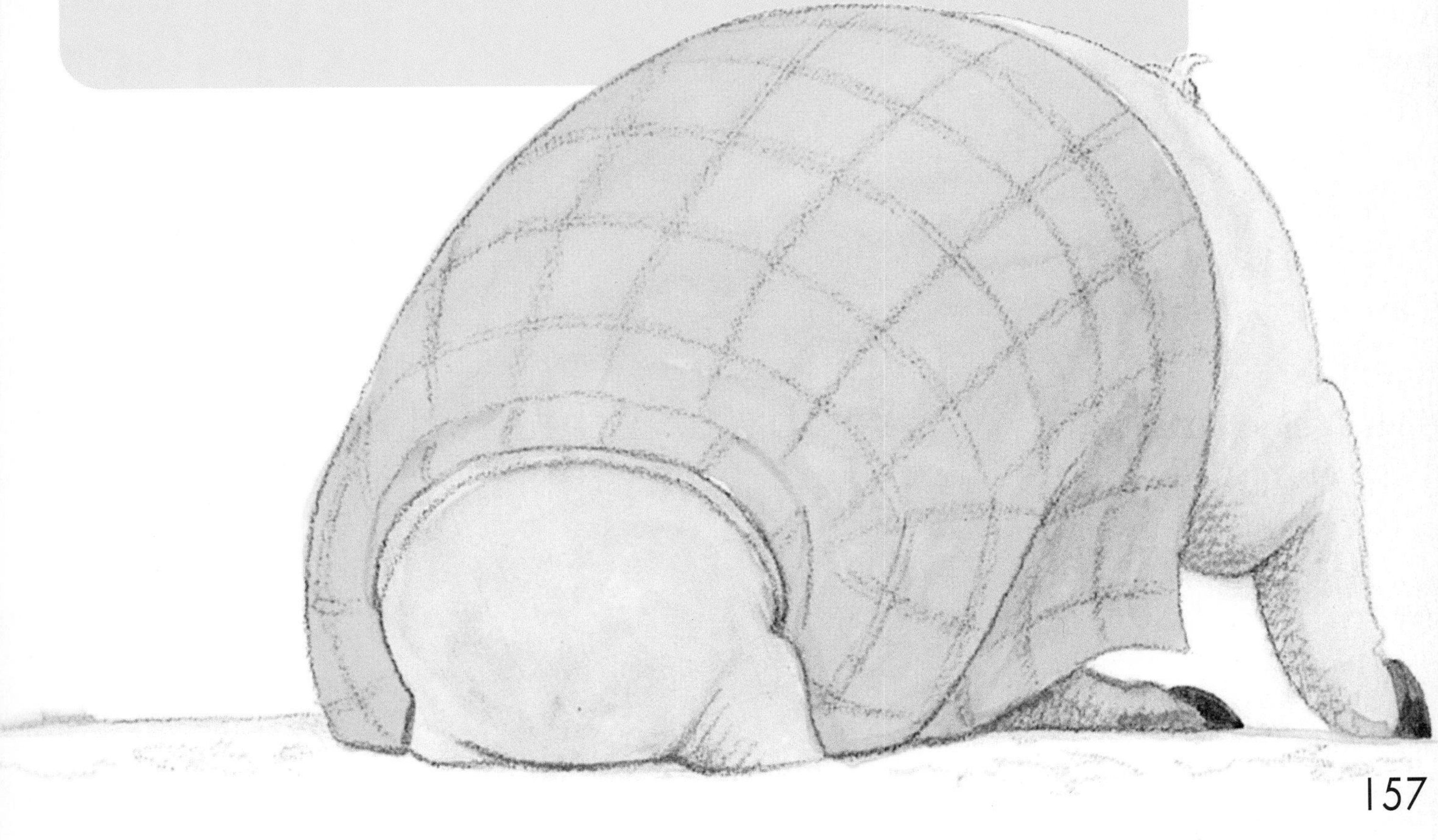

Genre

Fiction

Sometimes characters in fiction are funny.

Look for:

- **things a character does or says that are funny.**
- **other funny parts of the story.**

POPPLETON Everyday

by Cynthia Rylant
illustrated by Mark Teague

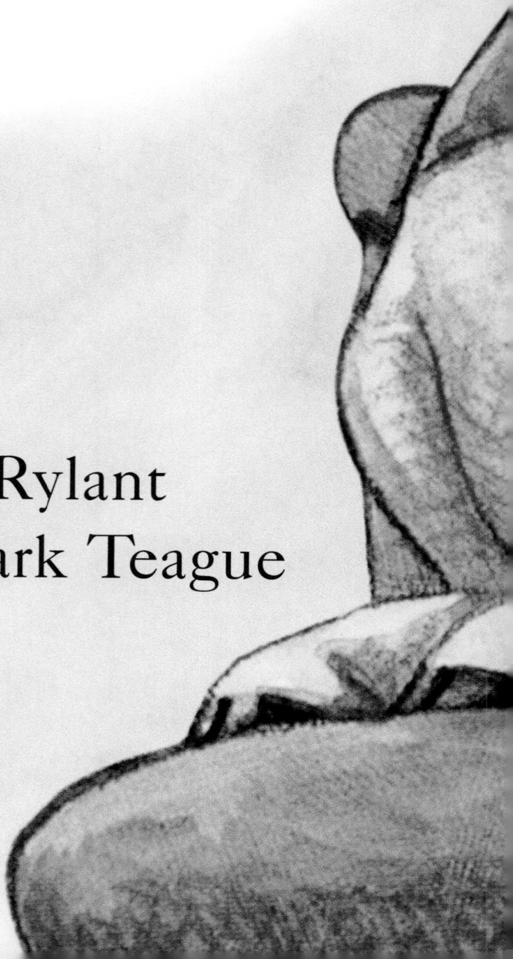

THE NEW BED

One day Poppleton decided
to buy a new bed.
He liked his old bed.
But he'd had it since he was a boy.
Now he wanted a grown-up bed.

So Poppleton went to the bed store.

“Do you have a bed just right for a pig?”
he asked the saleslady.
“Hmmm,” she said, looking Poppleton over.
“Right this way.”

Poppleton followed the saleslady
to the biggest bed in the store.

It was vast! It was enormous!
"It's just my size!" said Poppleton.

He climbed on to test the bed.

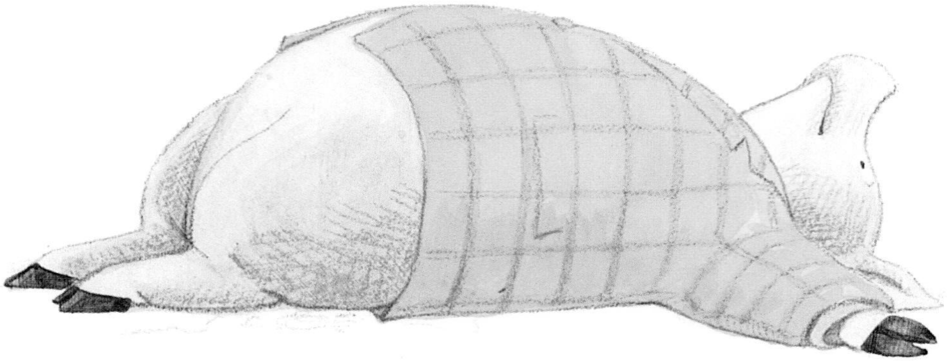

He lay on his back.

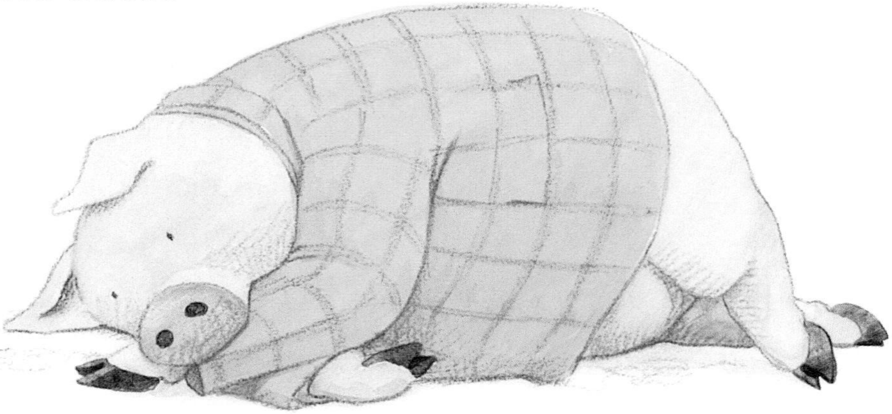

He lay on his side.

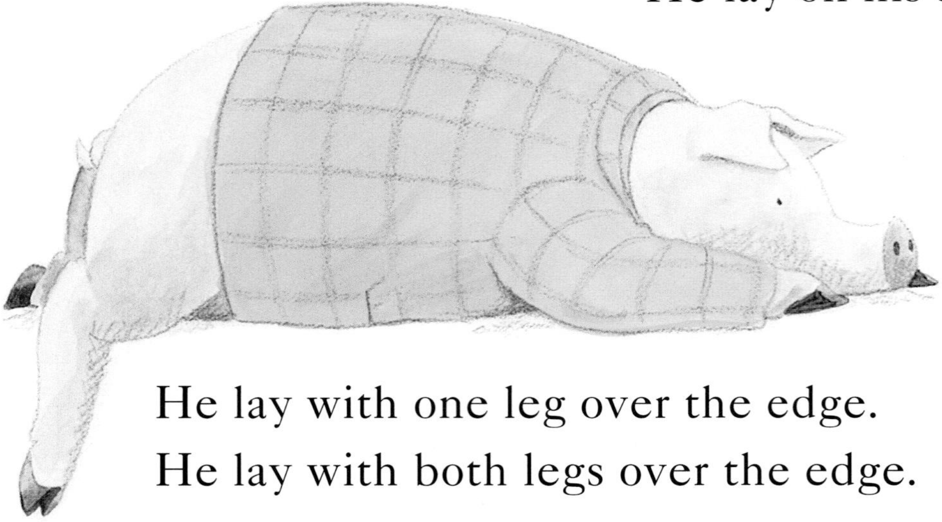

He lay with one leg over the edge.
He lay with both legs over the edge.

He lay on his head with his bottom in the air.

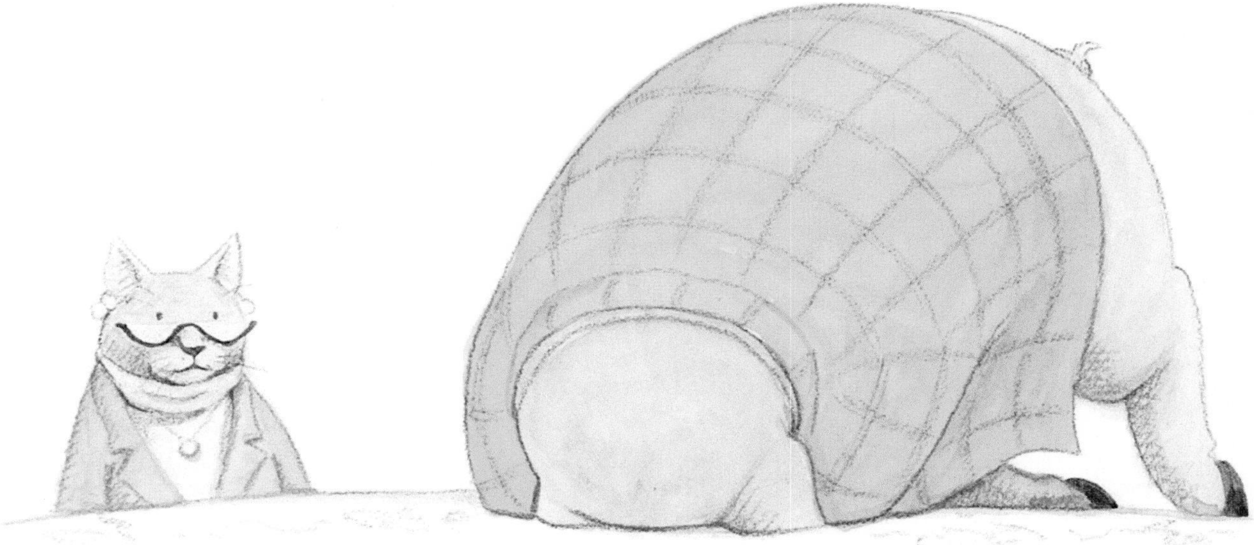

“How many different ways do you sleep?” asked the saleslady.
“About twenty,” said Poppleton.

“Do you have any books?” he asked.
The saleslady brought Poppleton a book.

Poppleton propped up some pillows
and read a few pages.
The saleslady looked at her watch.
"Do you want to buy the bed?"
she asked Poppleton.
"I don't know yet," said Poppleton.
"Do you have any crackers?"

The saleslady brought Poppleton
some crackers.
He got crumbs everywhere.
"Do you want the bed?"
asked the saleslady.

“I don’t know yet,” said Poppleton.
“Do you have a TV?”
The saleslady brought Poppleton a TV.
He watched a game show.

The saleslady checked her watch.
"Do you want the bed?"
she asked Poppleton.

"I don't know yet," said Poppleton.
"I have to check one more thing.
Do you have any bluebirds?"
"Pardon me?" said the saleslady.
"I always wake up to bluebirds,"
said Poppleton. "Do you have any?"

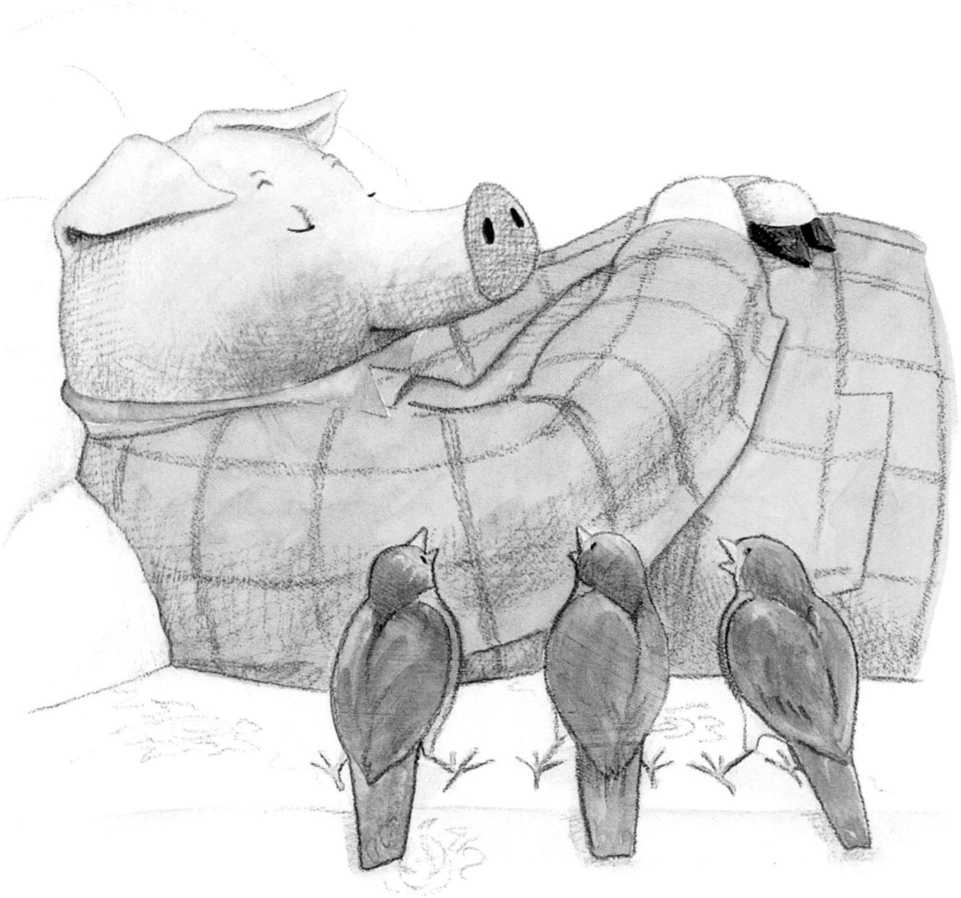

The saleslady went outside
and got three bluebirds to come in
and sing to Poppleton.
Poppleton lay with his eyes closed
and a big smile on his face.

"*Now* do you want the bed?"
asked the saleslady.

"Certainly!" said Poppleton.

And he picked up the book, the
crackers, the bluebirds, and the bed,
and happily went home.

BEDS! BEDS!
YES, WE'RE OPEN

Think and Respond

1. What does Poppleton do to test the bed before buying it?
2. Did you ever test something before making a decision? Tell what you did.
3. How does the saleslady feel about Poppleton? Give clues from the story that support your answer.
4. What did you learn about Poppleton's character from reading this story?
5. What did you like most about the story? What didn't you like? Tell why.

Meet the Author

CYNTHIA RYLANT

Cynthia Rylant grew up in the mountains of West Virginia. She spent a lot of time walking, playing, and thinking in the mountains. Now she likes to send copies of her books to her family. "They are all so proud and happy to receive them," she says. "It's nice to have a job people are so enthusiastic about!"

Cynthia Rylant

Teacher Read-Aloud

Meet the Illustrator

MARK TEAGUE

Mark Teague was working in a bookstore in New York City when he remembered how much he liked picture books as a child. He used to write and illustrate his own stories when he was a boy. He decided to try writing and illustrating children's books. He has illustrated more than fifteen of them.

Visit *The Learning Site!*
www.harcourtschool.com

Teacher Read-Aloud

▲ Poppleton Everyday

Making Connections

It's Bedtime

Make a list of things you do to get ready for bed. Make a card to show each thing. Draw and write about it. Tape the cards together and share your list.

Writing CONNECTION

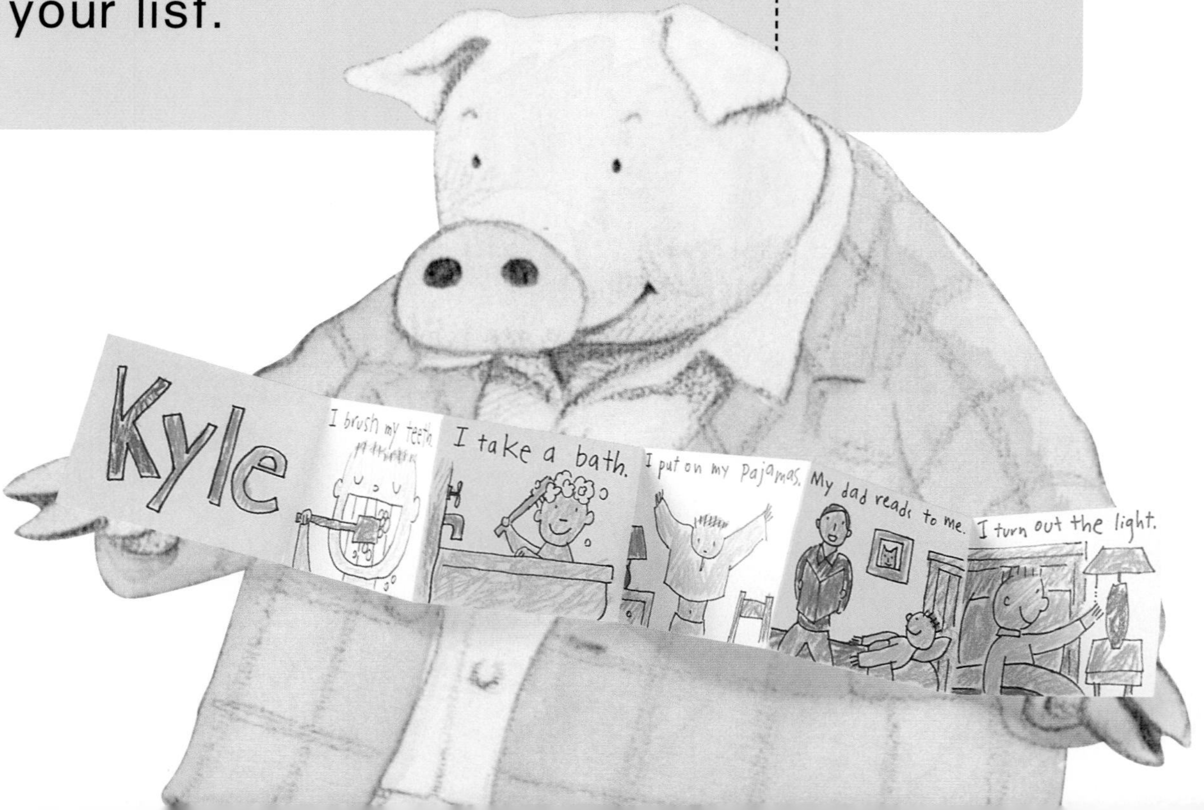

Where to Buy It

Social Studies CONNECTION

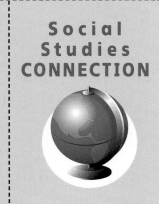

When Poppleton wanted a bed, he went to a bed store. Name other kinds of stores you go to for things you need. Make a list of different kinds of stores.

The New Bed

Art CONNECTION

Cut out a bed shape. Find or draw pictures of things Poppleton might have on his new bed. Glue your pictures to the bed and share your work.

Teacher Read-Aloud

▲ Poppleton Everyday

Words with u-e

Phonics Skill

When the letter **u** is followed by a consonant and **e**, it can stand for the long sound of **u** as in <u>cute</u> and <u>June</u>. Read these sentences.

> Poppleton got a **huge** bed.
> He will **use** it right away.
> Did you think that was a **cute** story?

Now read the words in the box. Each one has the long sound of **u**.

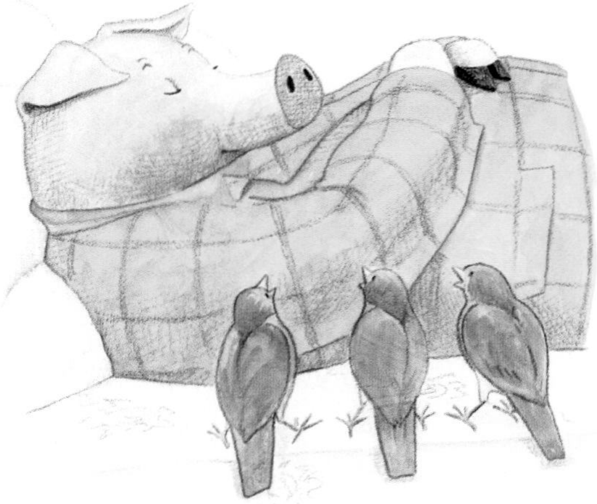

tune	**flute**	**cube**

Test Prep

Words with u-e

GEORGIA CRCT Tested Skill

1. Choose a word that names the picture.

mule ○ tube ○ mug ○

2. Choose a word that names the picture.

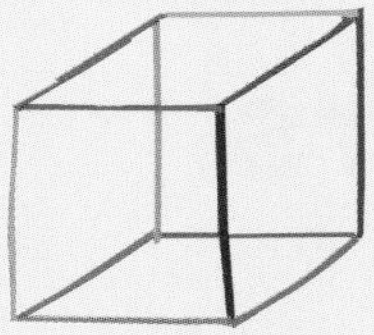

cut ○ prune ○ cube ○

Tip

Look at the words carefully. Read each word from beginning to end.

▲ Sleep Is for Everyone

Word Power

Words to Remember

afternoon

bicycle

carry

hours

parents

You ride your **bicycle** all **afternoon**. You **carry** your books to and from school. You play ball for **hours**. At night, your **parents** say, "Now you need to rest!"

Outstanding Science Trade Book

Genre

Nonfiction

In nonfiction pieces, an author gives information about a topic.

Look for:

- **Information about why sleep is important.**
- **Details and facts about sleep.**

SLEEP Is for Everyone

by Paul Showers

illustrated by Wendy Watson

When a horse goes to sleep, its eyelids go down.

When a chicken goes to sleep, its eyelids go up. When a snake sleeps, its eyes stay open. Snakes have no eyelids.

When you go to sleep, which way do your eyelids go?

An elephant can sleep standing up.

A pigeon sits down when it sleeps. Pigs lie down to sleep. So do dogs. So do you. Sometimes dogs curl up. So do cats. Cows don't.
Do you?

Like birds and animals, people have to sleep. Some people sleep more than others. Jonathan is only six weeks old. He sleeps most of the time. He only wakes up when he wants to eat—or have his diaper changed.

Caroline is two years old. She goes to bed right after her dinner. She sleeps all night, twelve hours or more. She takes a nap in the afternoon, too.

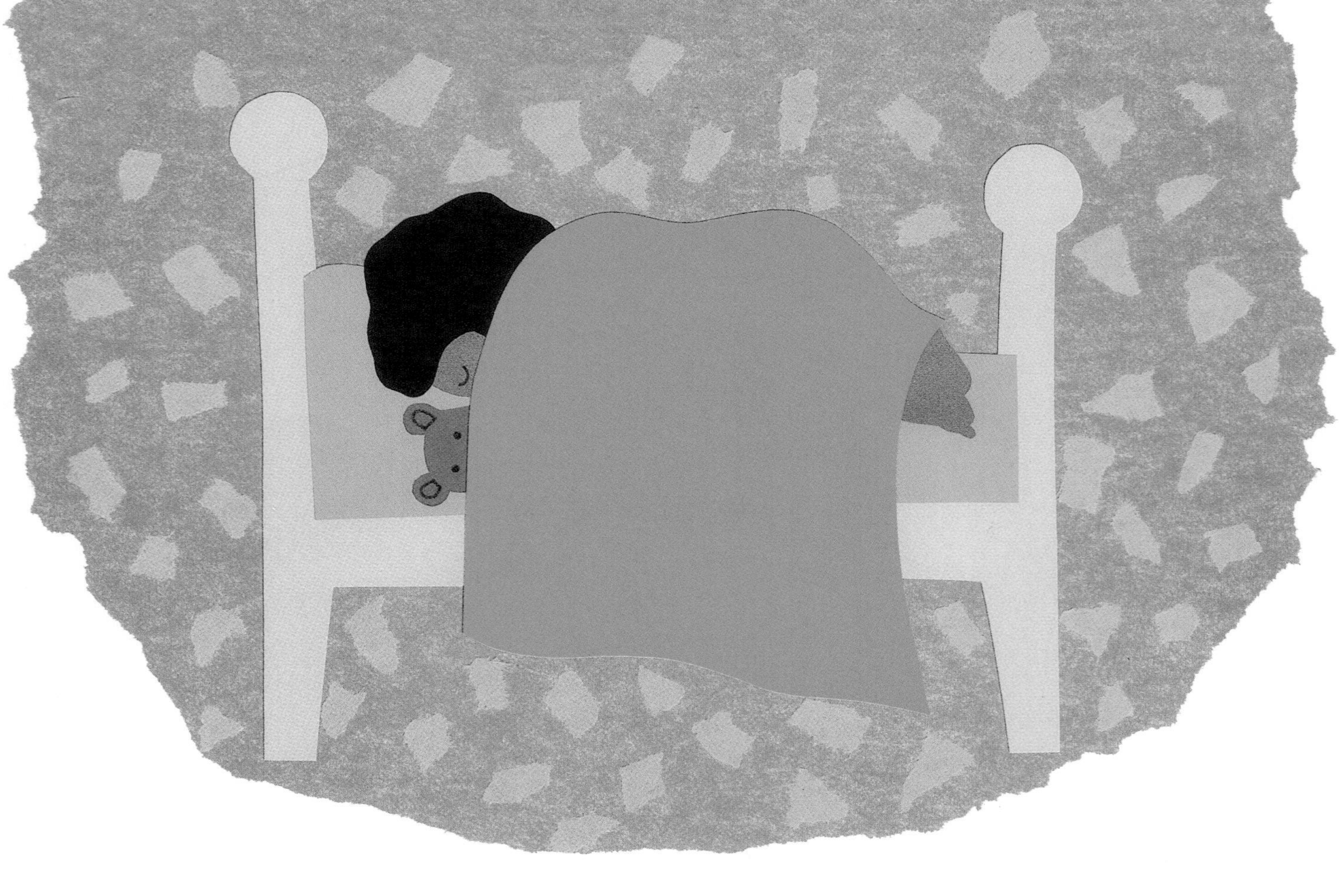

When Caroline doesn't get her nap, she is cranky. She cries. She throws things. But the next morning she feels fine—after she's had a good night's sleep.

When people are little, they are growing, and they need a lot of sleep. As they grow bigger and older, they need less sleep. Schoolchildren need to sleep about ten to twelve hours a night.

Most grown-ups need only seven or eight hours. But babies, children, and grown-ups—all of them need to have their sleep.

Every part of your body has to rest after it does its work. Your arms need to rest after they carry heavy bundles. When you run fast, your legs work hard. They get tired, and you have to rest them.

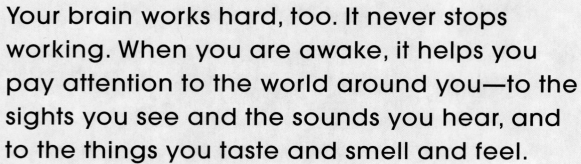

Your brain works hard, too. It never stops working. When you are awake, it helps you pay attention to the world around you—to the sights you see and the sounds you hear, and to the things you taste and smell and feel.

You can sit perfectly still and rest your arms and legs, but your brain isn't resting. It goes right on thinking as long as you are awake.

At night your brain needs a rest from thinking. It needs to turn off the world—the way you turn off the light when you go to bed. Sleep is the time when part of your brain takes a rest.

Sometimes it is hard to go to bed. Perhaps I want to watch something on TV. But my mother makes me go to bed. Sometimes she is cross with me. That's because she is tired. Sometimes I'm cross. That's because I'm tired.

Most of the time I go to bed when my parents tell me. It is warm under the covers. Sometimes I curl up. Or I stretch out and twist around. I yawn. I shut my eyes. I feel as if I am floating.

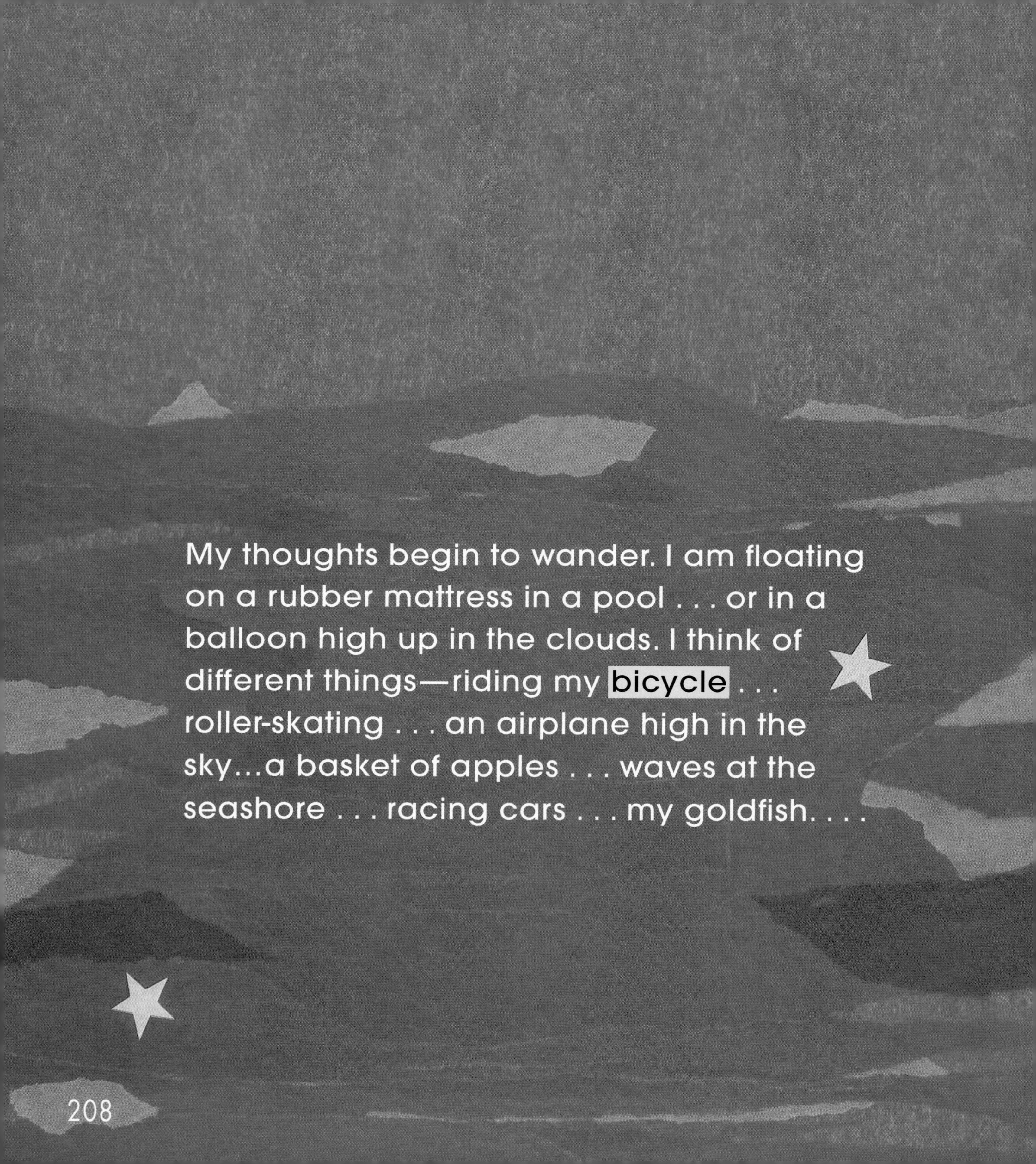

My thoughts begin to wander. I am floating on a rubber mattress in a pool . . . or in a balloon high up in the clouds. I think of different things—riding my bicycle . . . roller-skating . . . an airplane high in the sky...a basket of apples . . . waves at the seashore . . . racing cars . . . my goldfish. . . .

Soon I stop thinking. I am asleep.

Think and Respond

1. Is "Sleep Is for Everyone" a good title for this selection? Why?
2. Why is sleep important?
3. When does your brain get a rest from thinking?
4. Do you like to go to bed on time or stay up late? Tell why.
5. What can happen to children when they don't get enough sleep?

Teacher Read-Aloud

About the Author
Paul Showers

Paul Showers was a writer and editor at newspapers. Then he started writing science books for children. He liked to listen to children play. This gave him ideas for his books. Paul Showers knew how to make science fun for children.

Meet the Illustrator
Wendy Watson

Wendy Watson grew up in a large family. She is the oldest of eight children. As a child, she loved to draw. She made pictures, books, and cards and gave them to people as presents. The pictures for *Sleep Is for Everyone* are made from cut paper. Wendy Watson is also a musician. She plays the piano and the cello.

Teacher Read-Aloud Poem

Pretending

When you are in bed and it's cold outside,
do you ever pretend that you have to hide?
Do you curl up your toes?
Do you wrinkle your nose?
Do you make yourself little so none of you shows?

Do you pull the sheet over the whole of your face
and pretend you are in some faraway place?
Mother thinks you are sleeping,
but she does not know
that all tucked in the bed, you have places to go.

by Bobbi Katz

illustrated by Melissa Iwai

Teacher Read-Aloud

SLEEP
is for everyone

▲ Sleep Is for Everyone

Making Connections

Your Favorite Dream

We all dream while we sleep. Draw and write about a funny or interesting dream you have had. If you can't remember any dreams, make one up!

Writing CONNECTION

I dreamed
that I could fly.

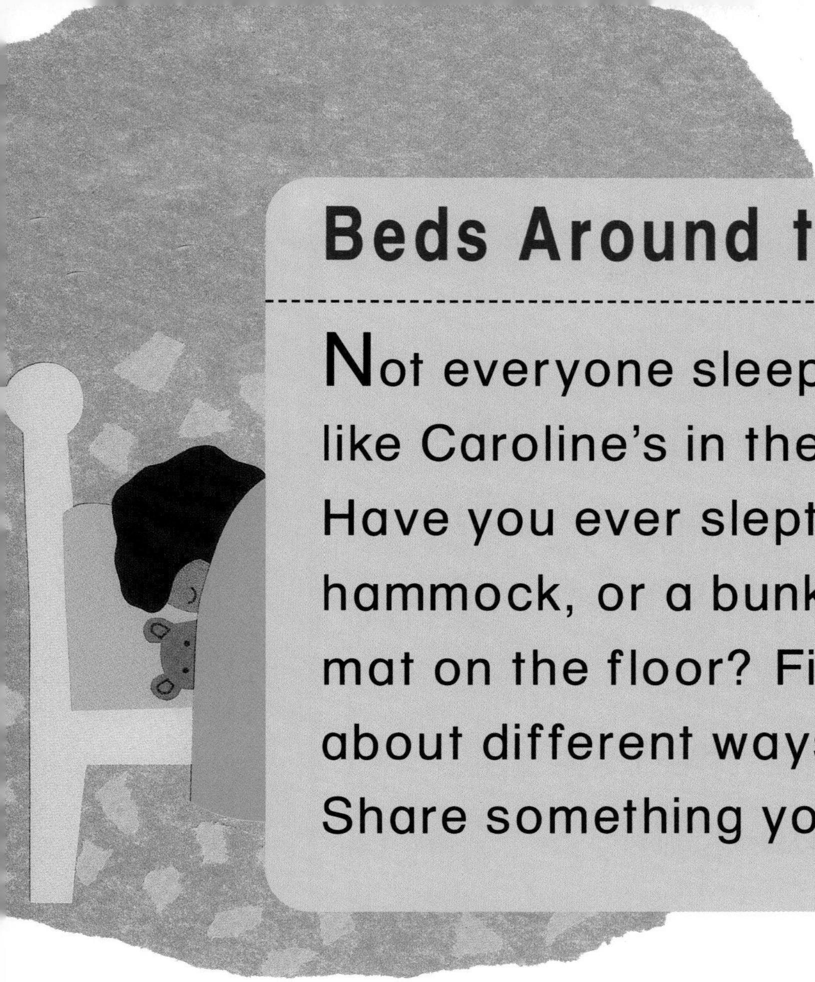

Beds Around the World

Not everyone sleeps in a bed like Caroline's in the story. Have you ever slept in a hammock, or a bunk bed, or a mat on the floor? Find out about different ways to sleep. Share something you learn.

Social Studies CONNECTION

A Lullaby

Sing a lullaby for baby Jonathan in the story.

Music CONNECTION

Rock-a-bye, Jonathan, in mother's lap,
Babies like you need a long nap.
Rock-a-bye, Jonathan, in the car seat.
Sleep till it's time to wake up and eat!

Teacher Read-Aloud

▲ Sleep Is for Everyone

Main Idea

Focus Skill

The **main idea** of a selection is what that selection is mostly about. Think about "Sleep Is for Everyone" as you read these sentences.

All people and animals need sleep. People need less sleep as they grow older.

Which sentence tells the **main idea**? Why do you think so?

Visit *The Learning Site!*
www.harcourtschool.com
See *Skills* and *Activities*

Test Prep
Main Idea

GEORGIA CRCT Tested Skill

Different animals sleep in different ways. Elephants and horses sleep standing up. Some birds sit down to sleep. Dogs lie down to sleep.

1. Which sentence best tells the main idea?

- ○ Some birds sit down to sleep.
- ○ Dogs lie down to sleep.
- ○ Different animals sleep in different ways.

Tip

Read the paragraph carefully. Which sentence tells what the whole paragraph is about?

▲ Baboon

Word Power

Words to Remember

against

careful

fire

quietly

shook

Baboon and his mother saw a **fire** in the forest. They watched it **quietly**.

Mother said, "We must be **careful**."

Then elephants walked by and **shook** the ground. Baboon leaned **against** his mother.

Booklist
Editors'
Choice

Genre

Informational Fiction

Some fiction stories give information about things in the real world.

Look for:

- **Parts of the story that are made-up.**
- **Information about different African animals.**

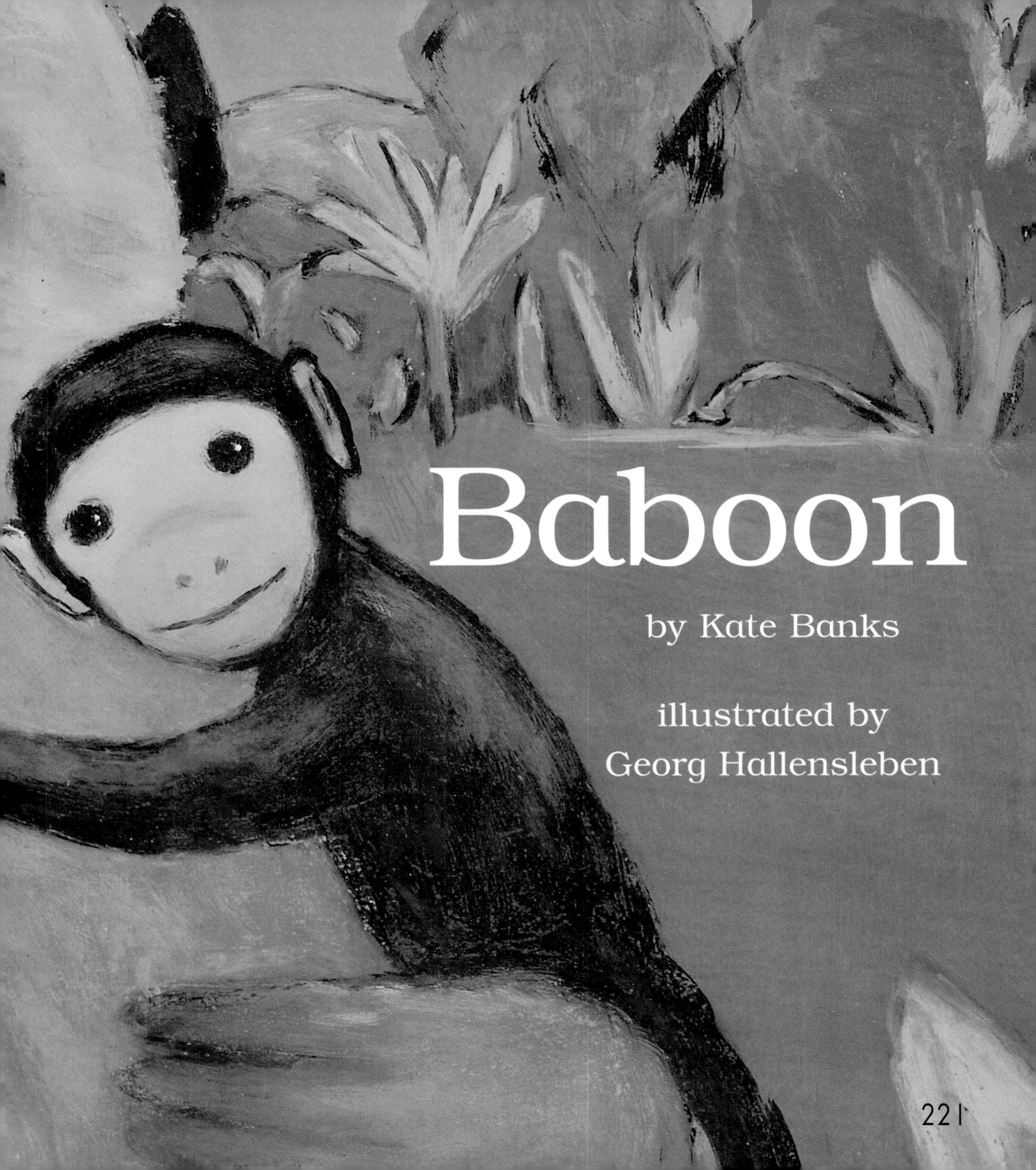

Baboon

by Kate Banks

illustrated by
Georg Hallensleben

Baboon opened his sleepy eyes.
Ahead was the great forest.
"Look," said his mother. "That is the world."
Baboon slid from his mother's back.
"So, the world is green," he said.
"Some of it," said his mother. And she led Baboon among the tall trees.

A turtle sat in the middle of the road.
Its eyes were closed and it barely moved.
Baboon watched and waited for the turtle
to pass. He waited a long time.
"The world is slow," he said.
"It can be," said his mother.

When the turtle had passed, Baboon followed his mother.
At the edge of the great forest, a fire burned in the bush.
Baboon moved close to the fire.
Soon he could feel its heat.
Baboon leaped backward.
"The world is hot!" he said.
"Not always," said his mother.

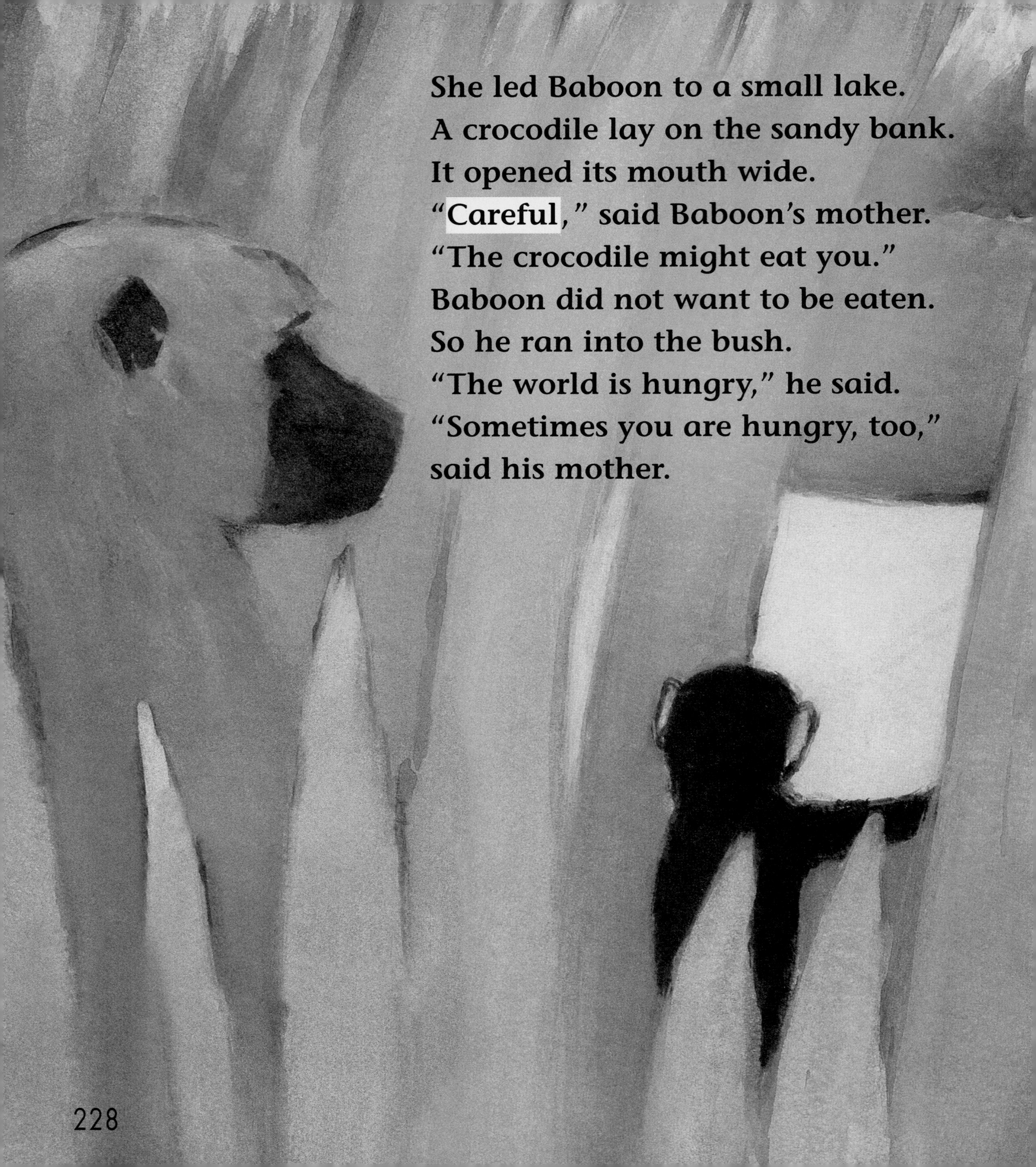

She led Baboon to a small lake.
A crocodile lay on the sandy bank.
It opened its mouth wide.
"Careful," said Baboon's mother.
"The crocodile might eat you."
Baboon did not want to be eaten.
So he ran into the bush.
"The world is hungry," he said.
"Sometimes you are hungry, too,"
said his mother.

Soon the elephants came, four by four. They thundered loud and shook the ground. A gazelle passed. He was not slow like the turtle, but quick and fast.

A rhinoceros darted out of the bushes.
He grunted at Baboon. Baboon was afraid.
"He will not hurt you," said his mother.

Baboon took his mother's hand, and they started across a field.
Baboon hid in the tall grass.
His mother hid, too. When they found each other, they lay down, side by side.
"The world is soft," said Baboon. And he was happy.

Baboon stretched and rolled over.
A bird flew by. A cloud passed
overhead. And Baboon fell asleep.
When he awoke, the sun was going down.
Baboon watched it disappear behind the trees.
"Come along," said his mother. And they
walked on.

Baboon followed his mother up
a tree.
Across from him sat a monkey.
He was like Baboon.
"Is he the world, too?" asked Baboon.
"He is," said his mother. "Just as
you are."
Baboon watched quietly.
Then he followed his mother down
the tree.

Now the elephants were huddled together. The gazelles were resting.
There was no more fire and the light was gone from the sky.
Baboon climbed onto his mother's back.
"The world is dark," he said.
"Sometimes," whispered his mother, carrying him home.

Baboon looked around.
He blinked.
Everything was black as far as he could see.
He laid his head against his mother's soft neck.
"The world is big," he said.
"Yes," said his mother softly. "The world is big."

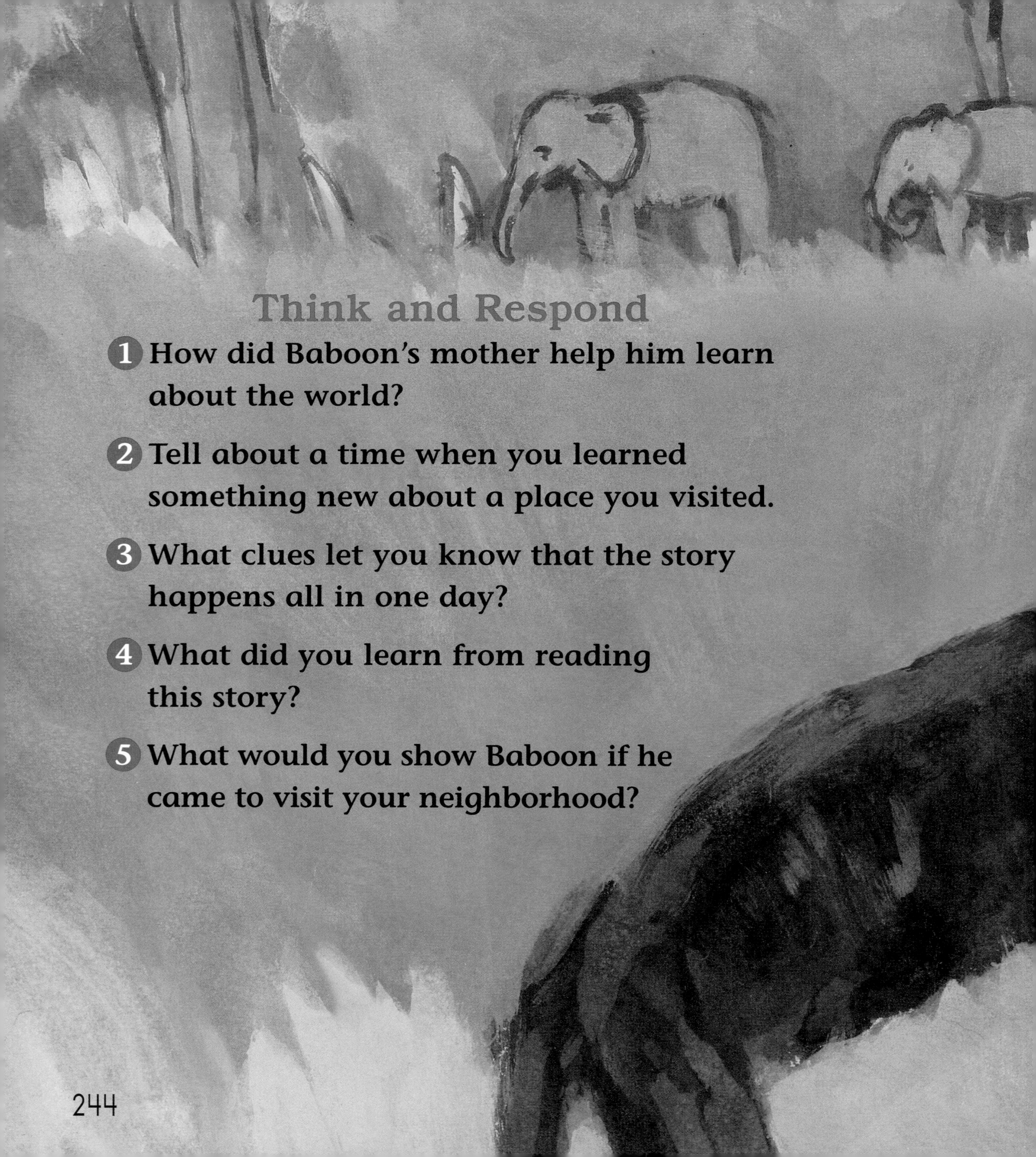

Think and Respond

1. How did Baboon's mother help him learn about the world?

2. Tell about a time when you learned something new about a place you visited.

3. What clues let you know that the story happens all in one day?

4. What did you learn from reading this story?

5. What would you show Baboon if he came to visit your neighborhood?

Teacher Read-Aloud

Meet the Author

Kate Banks

Kate Banks and her four-month-old son were looking at a picture of a mother baboon carrying her baby. That day, she began to think of the dialogue in "Baboon." Kate Banks likes watching, listening to, and being with children—she likes to write for them, too!

Kate Banks

Meet the Illustrator

Georg Hallensleben

Georg Hallensleben grew up in Germany. He loved riding his bike in the woods and drawing what he saw there. He used to bring his art supplies in a wooden case on his bike. He started drawing as a child and has never stopped!

Visit *The Learning Site!*
www.harcourtschool.com

Teacher Read-Aloud Magazine Article

Piggyback

Mother bears give their cubs a ride when they get tired. Do your parents give you piggyback rides?

The water is not safe for baby grebes. Big fish eat little chicks. Mom and dad make great lifeboats.

Ride

This frog has two tadpoles on its back. They are on their way to a pool of water. The tadpoles will grow up there.

Young lemurs hold on tight when they go piggybacking. Lemur parents swing from trees with their babies on board!

Teacher Read-Aloud

▲ Baboon

Making Connections

Make a Mobile

Baboon saw a **slow** turtle and a **fast** gazelle. Make a mobile of **opposites**. Cut out circles. Write opposite words on the two sides. Hang up your work!

Art CONNECTION

Mobile Sentences

Write pairs of sentences using words from your mobile. Draw pictures to go with them. Share your work.

Writing CONNECTION

Ice is cold.

This tea is hot.

Animals Baboon Saw

Baboon saw a monkey that looked a lot like him. Find out more about monkeys or another animal that Baboon saw. Use encyclopedia software or the Internet. Draw and write about the animal. Share your work.

Science/ Technology CONNECTION

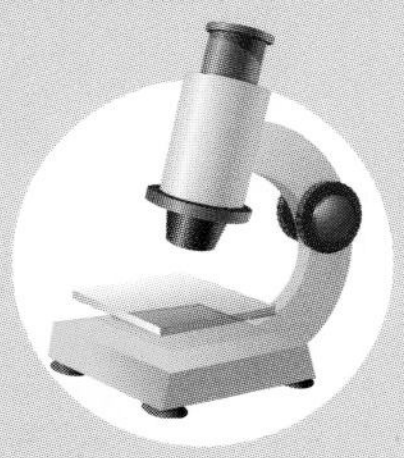

A rhinoceros has horns on its snout.

Teacher Read-Aloud

▲ Baboon

Plot

Focus Skill

You have learned that the **plot** of a story is what that story is about. Read these three sentences about the story "Baboon."

1. **Little by little, Baboon learns about the world around him.**
2. **Baboon sees the forest and learns that some of the world is green.**
3. **Baboon meets a monkey that looks a lot like him.**

Which sentence do you think best tells the plot of the whole story? Why?

Visit *The Learning Site!*
www.harcourtschool.com
See *Skills and Activities*

Test Prep
Plot

GEORGIA CRCT Tested Skill

The animals felt heat and saw flames. It was a forest fire! The birds flew away. Raccoon and his friends ran to the pond. "We're safe here," said Raccoon.

1. Which sentence best tells the plot?

- ○ Raccoon and his friends run to a pond.
- ○ The animals escape from a forest fire.
- ○ Animals feel the heat from a forest fire.

Tip

Remember that the plot is what happens in a story. Read all the sentences carefully before you answer.

The Writing Process

1. Prewrite

Draw or list some ideas. Choose one to write about.

2. Draft

Write about your idea. Don't worry about making mistakes.

3. Revise

Talk about your work. Make it better.

with
My dog is named ruff. He is brown ~~and~~
white ^ he does ^ tricks. I love my dog!
spots. lots of

4. Proofread

Read your story and fix the mistakes.

R with
My dog is named ~~r~~uff. He is brown ~~and~~
H
white ^ ~~h~~e does ^ tricks. I love my dog!
spots. lots of

5. Publish

Create a finished copy of your story. Share your writing.

My Dog
by Daniel Ruiz

My dog is named Ruff.
He is brown with white
spots. He does lots of
tricks. I love my dog!

Models for Writing

You can look at these writing models when you need to write something special.

Fantasy Story

Animal Games

One day some animals wanted to play. The giraffe wanted to play basketball. The cheetah wanted to race. The monkey wanted to play on the jungle gym. They took turns playing all the games. They all had fun.

Poem

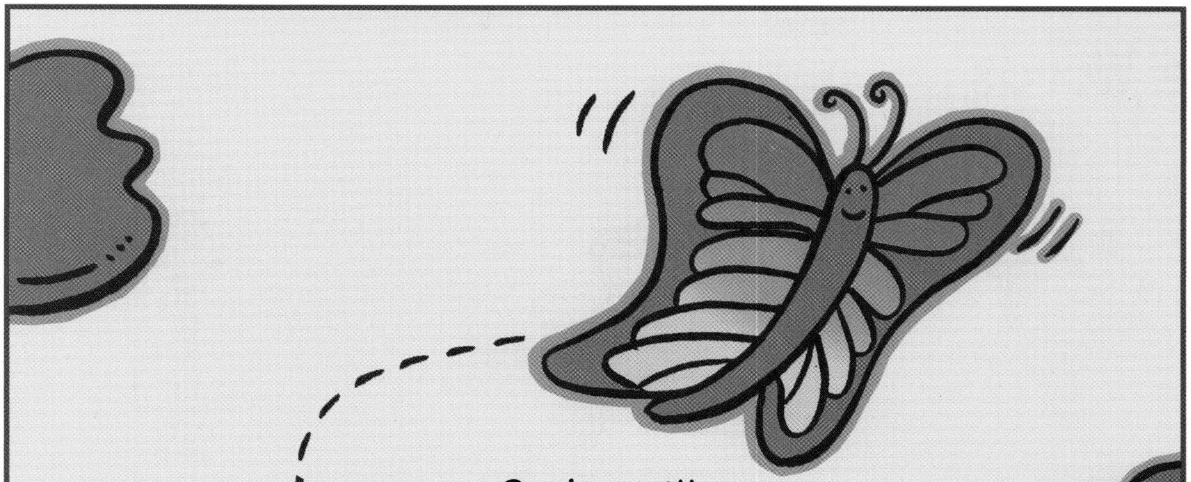

Caterpillar

by Sherry Hart

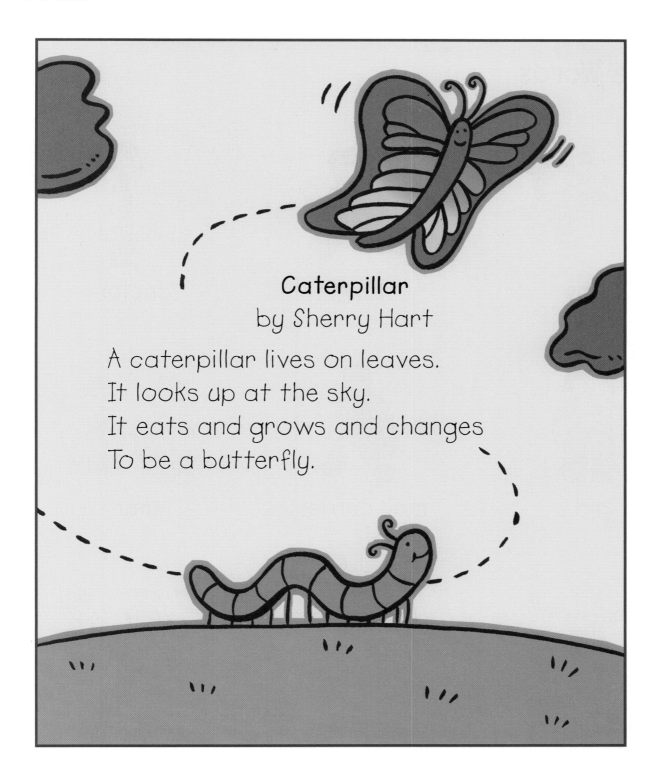

A caterpillar lives on leaves.
It looks up at the sky.
It eats and grows and changes
To be a butterfly.

Words for Writing

People Words

baby

boy

doctor

girl

mail carrier

man

police officer

teacher

woman

Verbs

draw

drive

eat

jump

play

read

run

skate

swing

walk

Words For Writing

Feeling Words

excited

happy

hungry

mad

proud

sad

scared

shy

sick

tired

Food Words

apple

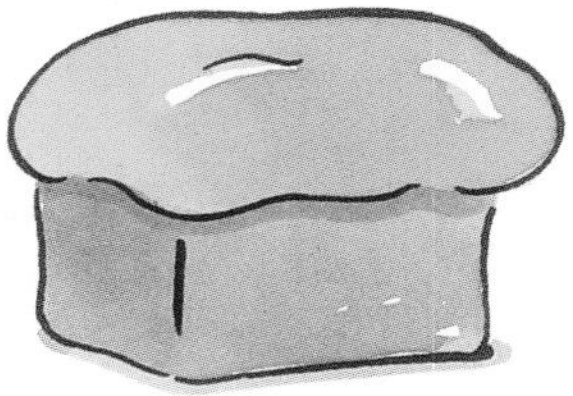

bread

cake

carrots

eggs

pancakes

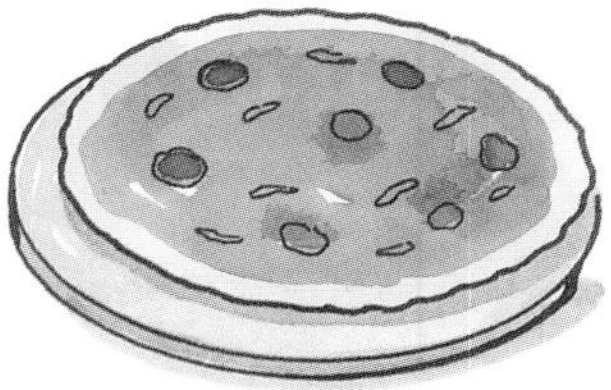

pizza

sandwich

spaghetti

taco

Glossary

What is a Glossary?

A glossary can help you read a word. You can look up the word and read it in a sentence. Some words have a picture to help you.

car•ry Albert can **carry** two bags.

A

a•fraid The tiger is **afraid** of the bunny.

af•ter•noon I have a snack in the **afternoon**.

a•gainst Stand up **against** the wall.

an•gry A leaky pen makes me **angry**.

afraid

angry

B

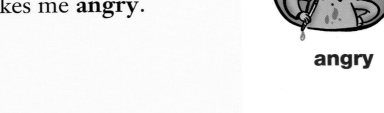

bi•cy•cle Lee rode her **bicycle** to the park.

both Can we have **both** kinds of ice cream?

boy The **boy** has brown hair.

brought The waiter **brought** us our pizza.

careful

C

care•ful Be **careful** with the flower vase!

carry

car•ry Albert can **carry** two bags.

caught Lilly **caught** a butterfly in a net.

cold I put on a coat when I am **cold**.

D

de•tec•tive A **detective** looks for clues.

detective

F

few We only have a **few** more tickets to the fair.

fire Dad lit a **fire** to help us stay warm.

fire

flew The airplane **flew** over the city.

floor

floor Clean the **floor** with a mop.

H

head He has no hair on his **head**.

head

hur•ried We **hurried** inside to get out of the rain.

J

join Do you want to **join** our game?

L

learn Let's **learn** a new song.

N

na•ture Animals, plants, and the sky are parts of **nature**.

near The park is **near** the school.

near•ly The bucket is **nearly** full.

noth•ing I have **nothing** in my pockets.

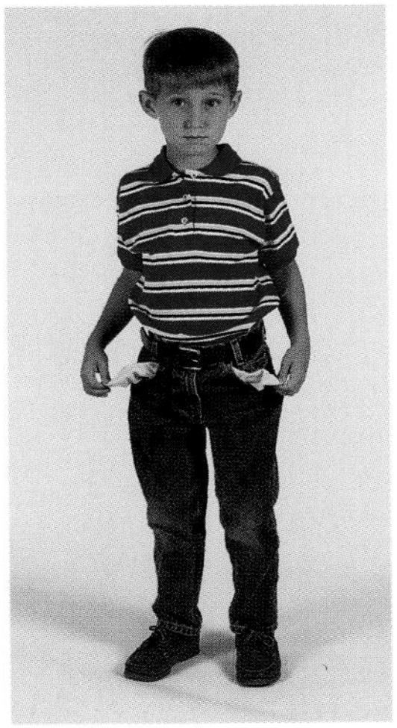

nothing

O

o•kay You fell down. Are you **okay**?

P

par•ents I call my **parents** Mama and Papa.

parents

piece

pulls

piece Do you want a **piece** of cake?

pulls The boy **pulls** the string to ring the bell.

Q

qui•et•ly Talk **quietly** in the library.

R

read Tammy **read** two books last night.

read•y Are you **ready** to go?

S

shook The baby **shook** her rattle.

son The boy is his dad's **son**.

son

sor•ry Abby was **sorry** she spilled the milk.

sorry

sure I am **sure** my answer is right.

T

thought Fred **thought** of a new game to play.

W

won•der I **wonder** how big that ship is.

Acknowledgments

For permission to reprint copyrighted material, grateful acknowledgment is made to the following sources:

The Blue Sky Press, an imprint of Scholastic Inc.: From "The New Bed" in *Poppleton Everyday* by Cynthia Rylant, illustrated by Mark Teague. Text copyright © 1998 by Cynthia Rylant; illustrations copyright © 1998 by Mark Teague.

Farrar, Straus and Giroux, LLC: Baboon by Kate Banks, illustrated by Georg Hallensleben. Text copyright © 1997 by Kate Banks; illustrations copyright © 1997 by Georg Hallensleben. *The Story of a Blue Bird* by Tomek Bogacki. Copyright © 1998 by Tomek Bogacki. *The Puddle* by David McPhail. Copyright © 1998 by David McPhail.

Nikki Grimes: "Time to Play" by Nikki Grimes. Text copyright © 1991 by Nikki Grimes.

HarperCollins Publishers: "The Corner" from *Frog and Toad All Year* by Arnold Lobel. Copyright © 1976 by Arnold Lobel. From *How to Be a Nature Detective* by Millicent E. Selsam, illustrated by Marlene Hill Donnelly. Text copyright © 1958, 1963, 1995 by Millicent E. Selsam; text copyright renewed © 1991 by Millicent E. Selsam; illustrations copyright © 1995 by Marlene Hill Donnelly. *Sleep Is for Everyone* by Paul Showers, illustrated by Wendy Watson. Text copyright © 1974 by Paul Showers; illustrations copyright © 1997 by Wendy Watson.

Bobbi Katz: "Pretending" by Bobbi Katz. Text copyright © 1973.

Lerner Publications, a Division of the Lerner Publishing Group: Fishing Bears by Ruth Berman, photographs by Lynn M. Stone. Text copyright © 1998 by Ruth Berman; photographs copyright © 1998 by Lynn M. Stone.

National Wildlife Federation: "Piggyback Ride" from *Your Big Backyard* Magazine, February 1998. Text copyright 1998 by the National Wildlife Federation.

Scholastic Inc.: Illustration by Floyd Cooper from *Pass It On: African-American Poetry for Children*, selected by Wade Hudson. Illustration copyright © 1993 by Floyd Cooper. Published by arrangement with Just Us Books, Inc.

Mark Warner: "Frogs in Trees?" by Mark Warner from *U. S. Kids*, a *Weekly Reader* Magazine, April 1989.

Photo Credits

Key: (t)=top; (b)=bottom; (c)=center; (l)=left; (r)=right

Page 60-63(all), Mark Warner; 65, Joe McDonald / Animals Animals; 68(tl)-84, Lynn M. Stone; 85(t), Lynn M. Stone; 85(inset), Glenn M. Oliver / Visuals Unlimited; 85(b), 86-87, Lynn M. Stone; 88, Rick McIntyre; 89-92, Lynn M. Stone; 93(t), Robin Buckley, courtesy Ruth Berman; 93(c), Brittany Stone / Lynn M. Stone; 93(b), Lynn M. Stone; 94, Rick McIntyre; 95, 96(both), Lynn M. Stone; 118, courtesy, HarperCollins; 121, Harcourt School Publishers; 149, Rick Friedman / Black Star; 180, Carlo Ontal; 181, 246-247, Black Star; 248(t), Tony Dawson; 248(b), Don Enger / Animals Animals; 249(t), Michael Fogden / DRK Photos; 249(b), Wolfgang Kaehler; 265(t), Will & Deni McIntyre / Photo Researchers, Inc.; 265(b), Chip Henderson / Index Stock; 266(t), Benelux Press / Index Stock; 266(b), Catherine Ledner / Stone; 267(t), Ken Kinzie / Harcourt; 267(b), Ron Chapple / FPG International; 268(t), Harcourt School Publishers; 268(b), Diaphor Agency / Index Stock; 269(t), Lawrence Migdale / Photo Researchers, Inc.; 269(b), Corbis.

Illustration Credits

Richard Cowdrey, Cover Art; Doug Bowles, 4-7; Tomek Bogacki, 8, 33, 36; Christine Mau, 34, 121, 214; C. D. Hullinger, 35; Liz Callen, 37, 250; Arnold Lobel, 38-59; Steve Björkman, 64, 95; Eldon Doty, 65, 67, 253; Ethan Long, 97; Marlene Hill Donnelly, 98-119, 122; Dona Turner, 120-121; Jo Lynn Alcorn, 123; David McPhail, 124-149, 152-154; Floyd Cooper, 150-151; Taia Morley, 155, 217; Mark Teague, 156-182, 184; Stacy Peterson, 185; Wendy Watson, 186-211, 215-216; Melissa Iwai, 212-213; Georg Hallensleben, 218-247, 252; Clare Schaumann, 251.

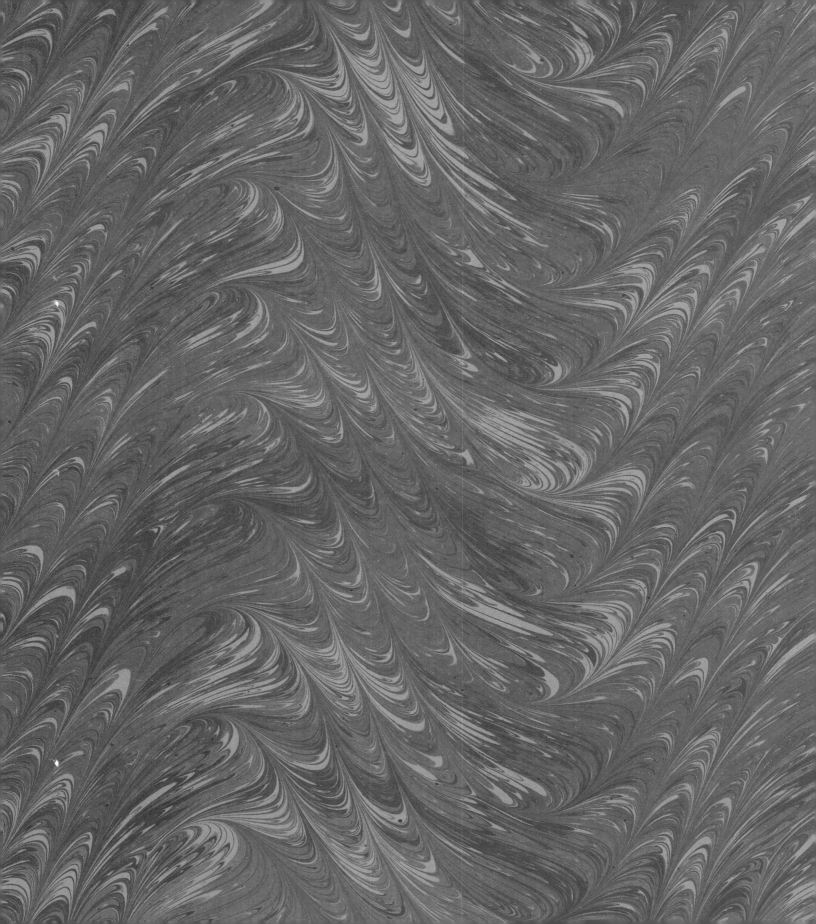

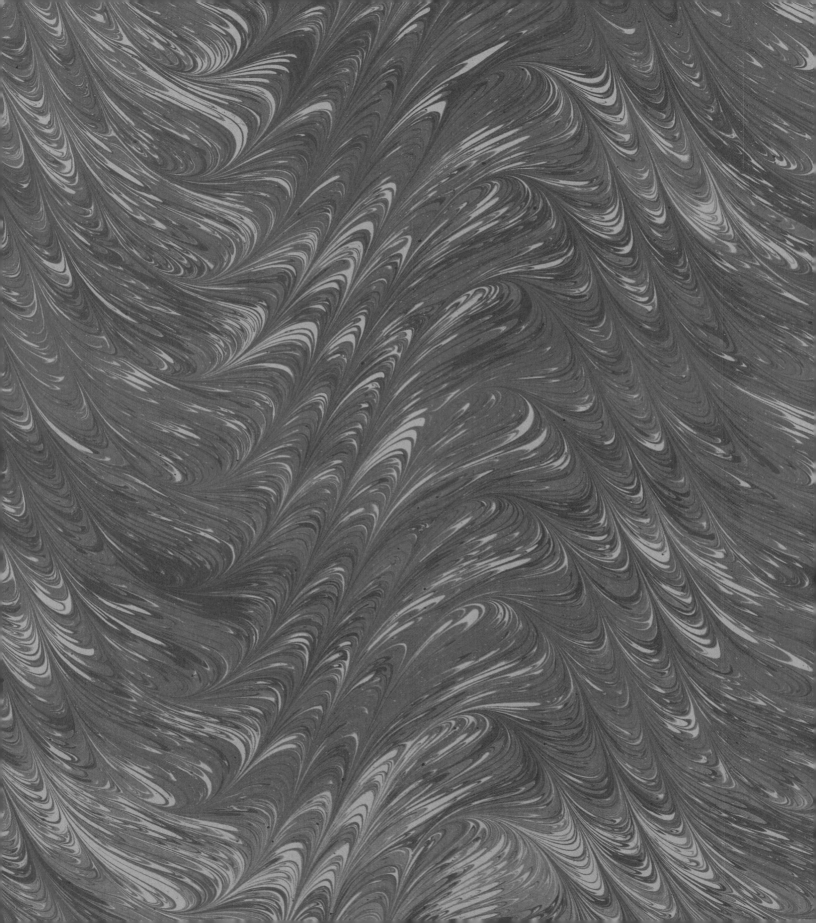